W9-BZT-315

QUICK & EASY
Dips!

Publications International, Ltd.

Pictured on the front cover (*clockwise top to bottom*): 7-Layer Dip (*page 38*), Chocolate Peanut Butter Fondue (*page 136*), and Cherry-Cheese Spread (*page 33*).

Pictured on the back cover: Picante Vegetable Dip (*page 67*).

ISBN-13: 978-1-68022-072-8

Library of Congress Control Number: 2015934784

Manufactured in China.

8 7 6 5 4 3 2 1

Microwave Cooking: Microwave ovens vary in wattage. Use the cooking times as guidelines and check for doneness before adding more time.

Preparation/Cooking Times: Preparation times are based on the approximate amount of time required to assemble the recipe before cooking, baking, chilling or serving. These times include preparation steps such as measuring, chopping and mixing. The fact that some preparations and cooking can be done simultaneously is taken into account. Preparation of optional ingredients and serving suggestions is not included.

Table of Contents

Hot & Hearty Dips

Hot Cheese-Chipotle Dip

2 **tablespoons unsalted butter**
1 **onion, chopped**
½ **red bell pepper, finely chopped**
1 **clove garlic, minced**
2 **tablespoons all-purpose flour**
1 **can (about 14 ounces) diced tomatoes, 2 tablespoons juice reserved**
1 **cup lager or pilsner beer, preferably Mexican**
1 **canned chipotle pepper in adobo sauce, minced, plus 1 teaspoon adobo sauce**
4 **cups (16 ounces) shredded Mexican-style cheese blend**
Chopped fresh cilantro (optional)
Tortilla chips

1. Melt butter in medium saucepan over medium heat. Add onion, bell pepper and garlic; cook and stir 5 minutes or until tender. Add flour; stir until well blended. Stir in tomatoes and reserved juice, lager, chipotle pepper and adobo sauce; bring to a boil. Reduce heat to low; simmer 5 minutes or until thickened.

2. Remove from heat. Stir in cheese blend, 1 cup at a time, until each addition is melted. If necessary, return to very low heat and stir just until melted. Sprinkle with cilantro. Serve warm with tortilla chips.

Makes 3 cups (8 servings)

Note: Don't overcook the cheese, or this dip will become gritty.

 For a zestier flavor, add more adobo sauce from the canned chipotle.

Spinach, Artichoke and Feta Dip

½ **cup thawed frozen chopped spinach**
1 **cup crumbled feta cheese**
½ **teaspoon black pepper**
1 **cup marinated artichokes, undrained**
   Pita chips or crackers

1. Place spinach in small microwavable bowl; microwave on HIGH 2 minutes.

2. Place cheese and pepper in food processor. Process 1 minute or until finely chopped. Add artichokes and spinach; process 30 seconds until well mixed but not puréed. Serve with pita chips or crackers.

Makes about 1½ cups

Tamale Pie Dip

2 **cups shredded Mexican-style cheese, divided**
1 **package (8 ounces) cream cheese**
1 **can (8 ounces) creamed corn**
1 **can (8 ounces) diced tomatoes**
½ **cup sour cream**
2 **cloves garlic, minced**
1 **teaspoon chili powder**
2 **cups diced cooked chicken**
1 **teaspoon olive oil**
  Optional toppings: sour cream, chopped or sliced black olives, diced avocado, sliced green onions or diced tomato
  Tortilla chips

1. Preheat oven to 325°F. Coat a 9-inch quiche dish or deep-dish pie plate with nonstick cooking spray; set aside.

2. Process 1 cup Mexican-style cheese, cream cheese, corn, tomatoes, sour cream, garlic and chili powder in food processor or blender until almost smooth. Stir in chicken by hand. Spoon mixture into prepared dish. Top with remaining 1 cup Mexican-style cheese. Drizzle with oil. Bake 45 minutes.

3. Garnish with toppings as desired. Serve with tortilla chips.

Makes about 5 cups

Ragú® Fondue

Prep Time: 10 minutes   **Cook Time:** 10 minutes

1 **jar (1 pound 8 ounces) RAGÚ® Old World Style® Pasta Sauce or RAGÚ® Organic Pasta Sauce**
   Assorted Dippers (cubed cheese, blanched vegetables, cooked tortellini, garlic bread cubes, meatballs)

Heat Pasta Sauce in 2-quart saucepan over medium heat. Turn into fondue pot or serving dish and serve warm with Assorted Dippers.

Makes 6 servings

Tip Keep pre-cut veggies and other dippers in plastic bags or containers in your refrigerator for unexpected guests.

Hot Crab-Cheddar Spread

1 **(8-ounce) container crabmeat, drained and shredded**

8 **ounces CABOT® Mild or Sharp Cheddar, grated (about 2 cups)**

½ **cup mayonnaise**

¼ **teaspoon Worcestershire sauce**

1. Preheat oven to 350°F.

2. In medium bowl, mix together all ingredients thoroughly. Transfer to small (1-quart) baking dish. Bake for 25 to 35 minutes, or until lightly browned on top and bubbling at edges. Serve with crackers or bread toasts.

Makes 8 to 10 servings

Baked Apricot Brie

1 **round (8 ounces) Brie cheese**
⅓ **cup apricot preserves**
2 **tablespoons sliced almonds**
   Cracked pepper or other assorted crackers

1. Preheat oven to 400°F. Place cheese in small baking pan. Spread top of cheese with preserves; sprinkle with almonds.

2. Bake 10 to 12 minutes or until cheese begins to melt and lose its shape. Serve hot with crackers. Refrigerate leftovers.

Makes 6 servings

Note: Brie is a soft-ripened, unpressed cheese made from cow's milk. It has a distinctive round shape, edible white rind and creamy yellow interior. Avoid Brie that has a chalky center (it is underripe) or a strong ammonia odor (it is overripe). The cheese should give slightly to pressure and have an evenly colored, barely moist rind.

Chipotle Beer Fondue

- **2 cups (8 ounces) shredded Swiss cheese**
- **2 cups (8 ounces) shredded Colby-Jack cheese**
- **1 cup (4 ounces) shredded Gouda cheese**
- **1 tablespoon cornstarch**
- **1 cup Mexican beer**
- **1 clove garlic, minced**
- **3 canned whole chipotle peppers in adobo sauce, minced**
- **½ cup chopped green onions**
- **⅛ teaspoon ground red pepper**
- **Tortillas and/or French bread cubes**
- **Cauliflower florets, carrot slices and/or bell pepper slices**

1. Toss Swiss, Colby-Jack and Gouda cheeses with cornstarch in large bowl; set aside.

2. Place beer and garlic in fondue pot or saucepan and bring to a boil over high heat. Reduce heat to low and slowly add cheese mixture, stirring constantly. Add chipotle peppers and green onions. Stir 2 to 3 minutes or until cheese is melted and mixture is smooth. Sprinkle with red pepper.

3. To serve, place fondue pot over low flame and serve with tortillas, French bread cubes, cauliflower florets, carrot slices or bell pepper slices. Use fondue forks or skewers for dipping.

Makes 8 to 10 servings

Tip If you do not have a fondue pot, prepare the fondue in a saucepan and transfer to a heated slow cooker for serving.

11

Chunky Pecan and Beef Dip

½ **cup pecan pieces**

3 **tablespoons thinly sliced green onions with tops**

1 **package (8 ounces) cream cheese, softened and cut into cubes**

½ **jar (2.2 ounces) dried beef, rinsed in hot water, drained and cut into ¼-inch pieces**

½ **teaspoon Italian seasoning**

Breadsticks, pita bread and assorted fresh vegetables for dipping

1. Spray bottom of small saucepan generously with nonstick cooking spray; heat over medium heat until hot. Add pecans and onions; cook over medium heat 3 to 5 minutes or until pecans are toasted and onions are tender.

2. Add ¼ cup hot water and cream cheese to saucepan; cook over medium-low heat until cheese is melted. Stir in dried beef and Italian seasoning; cook over medium-high heat, stirring constantly, until hot.

3. Spoon dip into bowl; sprinkle with additional green onion tops, if desired. Serve with dippers.

Makes 8 servings

Easy Cheese Fondue

1   **pound low-sodium Swiss cheese (Gruyère, Emmentaler or combination of both), shredded or cubed**
2   **tablespoons cornstarch**
1   **clove garlic, minced**
1   **cup HOLLAND HOUSE® White or White with Lemon Cooking Wine**
1   **tablespoon kirsch or cherry brandy (optional)**
    Pinch nutmeg
    Ground black pepper

1. In medium bowl, coat cheese with cornstarch; set aside. Rub inside of ceramic fondue pot or heavy saucepan with garlic; discard garlic. Bring wine to gentle simmer over medium heat. Gradually stir in cheese to ensure smooth fondue. Once smooth, stir in brandy, if desired. Garnish with nutmeg and pepper.

2. Serve with bite-sized chunks of French bread, broccoli, cauliflower, tart apples or pears. Spear with fondue forks or wooden skewers.

Makes 1¼ cups fondue

13

Baked Buffalo Chicken Dip

1 **container (8 ounces) light cream cheese spread**

¼ **cup reduced-fat crumbled blue cheese**

2 **cups chopped cooked chicken breast (about 8 ounces)**

3 **tablespoons light mayonnaise**

3 **tablespoons light sour cream**

¼ **to ½ cup hot pepper sauce**

1 **cup (4 ounces) shredded Monterey Jack cheese**

2 **tablespoons panko bread crumbs**

Assorted vegetable sticks and/or pita chips

1. Preheat oven to 400°F. Spray 1-quart casserole with nonstick cooking spray.

2. Combine cream cheese and blue cheese in medium saucepan; heat over medium heat until melted. Remove from heat. Stir in chicken, mayonnaise, sour cream and hot pepper sauce until combined.

3. Spread chicken mixture in prepared pan. Sprinkle with Monterey Jack cheese; top evenly with bread crumbs. Spray with cooking spray.

4. Bake 20 minutes or until lightly browned and heated through. Serve with assorted vegetable sticks and/or pita chips.

Makes 2 cups (about 16 servings)

Mexican Fondue with Spicy Soft Pretzel Bites

Prep Time: 5 minutes   **Start to Finish:** 15 minutes

Spicy Soft Pretzel Bites

- 1 **packet (1.25 ounces) ORTEGA® Taco Seasoning Mix**
- 1 **package (12 ounces) frozen soft pretzel bites (do not thaw)**
- 1 **cup water**

Mexican Fondue

- 1½ **cups prepared queso sauce or cheese sauce**
- ¼ **cup ORTEGA® Taco Sauce, any variety**

Preheat oven to 400°F.

Place seasoning mix in small bowl or resealable plastic food storage bag. Briefly dip frozen pretzel bites in water, shake off excess water, then toss with seasoning mix to coat. Place on baking pan; bake according to package directions.

Combine queso sauce and taco sauce in small saucepan over medium-low heat (or warm in microwave). Serve warm sauce with pretzel bites.

Makes 6 to 7 servings

 Can't find pretzel bites? Dunk whole soft pretzels or refrigerated bread sticks instead.

Simmering Fondue

1 **pound medium raw shrimp, peeled**

8 **ounces beef tenderloin steaks, cut into thin slices**

8 **ounces lamb loin, cut into thin slices**

2 **cups sliced mushrooms**

2 **cups sliced carrots**

2 **cups broccoli florets**

4 **cans (about 14 ounces each) fat-free reduced-sodium chicken broth**

½ **cup dry white wine**

1 **tablespoon chopped fresh parsley**

1 **teaspoon minced garlic**

½ **teaspoon dried thyme**

½ **teaspoon dried rosemary**

1. Arrange shrimp, beef, lamb, mushrooms, carrots and broccoli on large serving platter or in individual bowls.

2. Combine broth, wine, parsley, garlic, thyme and rosemary in large saucepan. Bring to a boil over high heat. Remove from heat; strain broth into electric wok. Return to a simmer over high heat.

3. Thread any combination of shrimp, meat and vegetables onto bamboo skewer or use fondue fork. Cook in broth 2 to 3 minutes.

Makes 4 servings

Spicy Sausage Queso

Prep Time: 25 minutes   **Cook Time:** 8 minutes

1 **package (16 ounces) JOHNSONVILLE® Ground Italian Sausage**
2 **pounds pasteurized process cheese product, cubed**
1 **jar (16 ounces) chunky salsa**
1 **tablespoon fennel seed, crushed**
2 **teaspoons garlic powder**
1 **teaspoon anise seed, crushed**
¼ **teaspoon dried basil**
  Garlic toast

Cook sausage in large skillet over medium-high heat, stirring to break meat into bite-size pieces, 5 to 7 minutes or until no longer pink. Set aside.

Microwave cheese in large bowl 6 minutes or until melted, stirring well every 2 minutes.

Transfer sausage from skillet to bowl with cheese with slotted spoon. Stir in salsa, fennel seed, garlic powder, anise seed and dried basil. Microwave 2 minutes longer or until heated through. Serve immediately with garlic toast.

Makes 24 servings

Sara's Guiltless Artichoke Dip

8 **light garlic-and-herb spreadable cheese wedges**

1 **can (about 14 ounces) artichokes packed in water, rinsed, drained and coarsely chopped**

½ **cup (2 ounces) shredded reduced-fat mozzarella cheese**

¼ **cup shredded Parmesan cheese**

1 **tablespoon light sour cream, plus additional if necessary**

2 **teaspoons fresh lemon juice**

¼ **teaspoon ground red pepper**

Assorted vegetable sticks, pretzel chips and/or crackers

Microwave Directions

1. Stir cheese wedges in medium microwavable bowl until smooth. Add artichokes, mozzarella cheese, Parmesan cheese, 1 tablespoon sour cream, lemon juice and red pepper. Add additional sour cream, if necessary, to thin dip to desired consistency.

2. Microwave on HIGH 1 minute; stir. Microwave at 30-second intervals until heated through, stirring after each interval.

3. Serve with assorted vegetable sticks, pretzel chips and/or crackers.

Makes 2 cups (about 16 servings)

18

Hot Crab Spread

Prep Time: 10 minutes   **Cook Time:** 30 to 35 minutes

1   **package (8 ounces) reduced-fat cream cheese, softened**

1   **can (6 ounces) crabmeat**

¼   **cup nonfat plain yogurt**

2   **tablespoons finely chopped green onion**

1   **tablespoon MRS. DASH® Garlic & Herb Seasoning Blend**

1   **tablespoon fresh lemon juice**

2   **teaspoons fresh parsley, chopped**

2   **tablespoons grated Parmesan cheese**

1. Preheat oven to 375°F.

2. Combine all ingredients except Parmesan cheese in medium bowl; mix well.

3. Spray baking dish with vegetable cooking spray.

4. Spoon mixture into prepared baking dish.

5. Sprinkle with Parmesan cheese.

6. Bake 30 to 35 minutes.

Makes 12 servings

Pretzel Dippers

⅓ **cup spicy brown mustard**

3 **tablespoons whipped butter**

2 **tablespoons mayonnaise**

1 **package frozen soft pretzels (6 pretzels)**

24 **thin slices salami, cut into halves**

10 **ounces Swiss cheese, cut into scant ½-inch cubes**

Microwave Directions

1. Whisk mustard, butter and mayonnaise in small bowl until well blended.

2. Dampen pretzels with water and sprinkle with salt from package. Microwave 2 minutes or until pretzels are warm.

3. Cut each pretzel into 8 pieces. Wrap half slice of salami around each pretzel piece; top with cheese cube and secure with toothpick. Serve with mustard sauce for dipping.

Makes 48 pieces

Pumpkin Chile Cheese Dip

1 **tablespoon butter**

¼ **cup finely chopped green bell pepper**

2 **tablespoons finely chopped onion**

1 **can (10¾ ounces) condensed nacho cheese soup,* undiluted**

1 **cup solid-pack pumpkin**

½ **cup half-and-half**

1 **to 2 teaspoons minced canned chipotle peppers in adobo sauce**

¼ **teaspoon salt**

Tortilla chips and/or vegetables

*If nacho cheese soup is unavailable, substitute Cheddar cheese soup and add additional ½ teaspoon chipotle pepper.

1. Melt butter in medium saucepan over medium heat. Add bell pepper and onion; cook and stir 3 minutes or until tender.

2. Reduce heat to low. Stir in soup, pumpkin, half-and-half, 1 teaspoon chipotle pepper and salt; cook 10 minutes, stirring frequently. Taste and add additional chipotle pepper, if desired. Serve warm with tortilla chips and vegetables for dipping.

Makes about 2 cups

Note: Two teaspoons of chipotle pepper will make the dip very spicy. Start with 1 teaspoon and taste before adding additional chipotle pepper.

Quick Cheese Fondue

Prep Time: 5 minutes   **Cook Time:** 10 minutes

1　**can (10½ ounces) Campbell's® Condensed French Onion Soup**
¼　**cup dry sherry**
1　**package (8 ounces) cream cheese, softened**
1　**cup shredded Gruyère cheese (about 4 ounces)**
　　Assorted Dippers: **French bread cubes, warm Pepperidge Farm® Garlic Bread cubes, cooked mini meatballs, deli roast beef cubes, steamed baby red potato halves**

1. Heat the soup and sherry in a 3-quart saucepan over medium-high heat for 5 minutes. Stir in the cream cheese and Gruyère cheese. Reduce the heat to low. Cook and stir until the cheeses are melted.

2. Pour the cheese mixture into a fondue pot or slow cooker. Serve warm with *Assorted Dippers*.

Makes 20 servings

Kitchen Tip: To soften the cream cheese, remove from the wrapper and place onto a microwave-safe plate. Microwave on HIGH for 15 seconds.

Warm Salsa & Goat Cheese Dip

Nonstick cooking spray
8 (10-inch) assorted flavor flour tortillas
   Salt
1¼ cups medium salsa
1 log (4 ounces) goat cheese (not crumbles)
2 tablespoons coarsely chopped fresh cilantro

1. Preheat oven to 350°F. Spray baking sheets with cooking spray.

2. Use 2- and 3-inch leaf-shaped cookie cutters to cut shapes from tortillas. Lightly spray tortillas with cooking spray. Arrange on prepared baking sheets; season with salt to taste. Bake 7 minutes or until edges begin to brown. Remove to wire rack to cool completely.

3. Pour salsa into 9-inch pie plate or 2-quart gratin dish. Cut goat cheese crosswise into 5 pieces; arrange over salsa.

4. Bake about 20 minutes or until salsa is bubbly and cheese is heated through. Sprinkle with cilantro. Serve warm with tortilla chips.

Makes about 8 servings

Warm Crab and Beer Dip

12 **ounces cream cheese, softened**
½ **cup finely chopped red bell pepper**
½ **cup mayonnaise**
½ **cup beer**
¼ **cup finely chopped onion**
¼ **cup chopped fresh parsley**
1 **egg**
1 **teaspoon hot pepper sauce**
¼ **teaspoon salt**
12 **ounces crabmeat***
   Pita chips

*Pick out and discard any shell or cartilage from crabmeat.

1. Preheat oven to 375°F. Spray 4-cup baking dish with nonstick cooking spray.

2. Combine cream cheese, bell pepper, mayonnaise, beer, onion, parsley, egg, hot pepper sauce and salt in medium bowl; stir to blend. Fold in crabmeat. Place in prepared dish.

3. Bake 35 minutes or until bubbly and browned on top. Let stand 10 minutes. Serve with pita chips.

Makes 8 servings

Easiest Three-Cheese Fondue

- 1 **tablespoon margarine**
- ¼ **cup finely chopped onion**
- 2 **cloves garlic, minced**
- 1 **tablespoon all-purpose flour**
- ¾ **cup reduced-fat (2%) milk**
- 2 **cups (8 ounces) shredded mild or sharp Cheddar cheese**
- 1 **package (3 ounces) cream cheese, cut into cubes**
- ½ **cup (2 ounces) crumbled blue cheese**
- ⅛ **teaspoon ground red pepper**
- 4 **to 6 drops hot pepper sauce**
  Breadsticks and assorted fresh vegetables for dipping

1. Heat margarine in small saucepan over medium heat until melted. Add onion and garlic; cook and stir 2 to 3 minutes or until tender. Stir in flour; cook 2 minutes, stirring constantly.

2. Stir milk into saucepan; bring to a boil. Boil, stirring constantly, about 1 minute or until thickened. Reduce heat to low. Add cheeses; cook and stir until melted. Stir in red pepper and pepper sauce. Pour fondue into serving dish. Serve with dippers.

Makes 8 servings

Lighten Up: To reduce the total fat in this recipe, replace the Cheddar cheese and cream cheese with reduced-fat Cheddar and cream cheeses.

Crumb-Topped Cheesy Artichoke Dip

Prep Time: 15 minutes   **Cook Time:** 30 minutes

1 **cup coarsely torn fresh bread crumbs**
¼ **cup grated Parmesan cheese**
¼ **cup coarsely chopped flat-leaf parsley (optional)**
1 **can (14 ounces) artichoke hearts, drained and chopped**
1 **package KNORR® Leek recipe mix**
1 **container (16 ounces) sour cream**
1 **cup shredded Swiss or mozzarella cheese (about 4 ounces)**
½ **cup HELLMANN'S® or BEST FOODS® Real Mayonnaise**

1. Preheat oven to 375°F.

2. Combine bread crumbs, Parmesan cheese and parsley in small bowl; set aside.

3. Combine artichoke hearts, KNORR® Leek recipe mix, sour cream, Swiss cheese and HELLMANN'S® or BEST FOODS® Real Mayonnaise in 5- to 6-cup casserole.

4. Top with bread crumb mixture.

5. Bake, uncovered, 30 minutes or until golden and heated through. Serve, if desired, with your favorite dippers.

Makes 4½ cups dip

Substitution: Also terrific with HELLMANN'S® or BEST FOODS® Light Mayonnaise or Mayonnaise Dressing with Olive Oil.

Spiced Beer Fondue

1 **bottle (12 ounces) light-colored beer, such as ale or lager**
2 **cups (8 ounces) shredded Gruyère cheese**
1 **cup (4 ounces) shredded Cheddar cheese**
2 **tablespoons all-purpose flour**
1 **teaspoon coarse grain mustard**
¼ **teaspoon salt**
⅛ **teaspoon ground red pepper**
¼ **teaspoon ground nutmeg**
Apple slices, bread cubes, cooked potato pieces and/or fresh vegetables

1. Bring beer to a boil in medium saucepan. Reduce heat to medium-low. Simmer 5 minutes or until it stops foaming. Reduce heat to low.

2. Toss cheeses with flour in medium bowl. Gradually add cheese mixture to beer, stirring constantly. Add mustard, salt and red pepper. Cook, stirring constantly, until cheese is melted. Transfer to fondue pot over low heat; sprinkle with nutmeg. Serve with apple slices, bread cubes, potato pieces and/or vegetables.

Makes 4 servings

 Tip Stirring constantly while cooking the fondue is essential. If left still over heat, the cheese will easily burn.

Cold Dips & Spreads

Potted Beer and Cheddar

- 8 ounces cream cheese, softened
- 4 tablespoons CABOT® Unsalted Butter, softened
- 4 cups grated CABOT® Sharp Cheddar (about 1 pound)
- 1 tablespoon minced fresh chives
- 1 tablespoon chopped fresh parsley
- 1 teaspoon Worcestershire sauce
- 1 teaspoon Dijon mustard
- 1 teaspoon prepared horseradish
- ½ clove garlic, minced
- ¼ teaspoon ground black pepper
- 2 to 3 drops hot pepper sauce
- ¼ to ½ cup flat beer

1. With electric mixer, beat together cream cheese and butter until well blended. Mix in cheese.

2. Mix in all remaining ingredients except beer. Add enough beer to make spread of desired consistency (mixture will thicken further after chilling).

3. Pack into earthenware crock or other ceramic dish; cover and refrigerate for several hours to allow flavors to blend. Serve with apple slices and dark rye bread or crackers.

Makes about 3 cups

Note: Spread can be made several weeks in advance.

Spicy Shrimp Cocktail Spread

Prep Time: 10 minutes   **Chill Time:** 6 hours

- 1 **envelope unflavored gelatin**
- ¼ **cup cold water**
- 1 **can (10¾ ounces) Campbell's® Condensed Tomato Soup (Regular or Healthy Request®)**
- 1 **package (8 ounces) cream cheese, cut into pieces**
- 1 **cup mayonnaise**
- 2 **tablespoons prepared horseradish**
- 1 **teaspoon hot pepper sauce**
- 2 **stalks celery, chopped (about 1 cup)**
- 1 **large onion, diced (about 1 cup)**
- 3 **cans (4 to 6 ounces each) baby shrimp, drained**
   Assorted Pepperidge Farm® Crackers

1. Sprinkle the gelatin over the water in a 2-quart saucepan. Let stand for 3 minutes or until the gelatin softens.

2. Stir the soup into the saucepan. Cook and stir over medium heat until the gelatin dissolves. Add the cream cheese and stir until the cheese melts. Remove from the heat.

3. Spoon the soup mixture, mayonnaise, horseradish, hot pepper sauce, celery, onion and shrimp into an electric food processor or blender. Cover and process until smooth. Pour mixture into a 6-cup mold. Cover and refrigerate for at least 6 hours or until the mixture is firm.

4. Invert and unmold the mixture onto serving plate. Serve with the crackers.

Makes 6 cups

Creamy Vegetable Dip

2 **packages (8 ounces each) light cream cheese, softened**

½ **cup** *each* **finely chopped broccoli and shredded carrot**

2 **tablespoons fat-free (skim) milk**

2 **tablespoons sliced green onion**

1 **tablespoon lemon juice**

1 **teaspoon grated lemon peel**

½ **teaspoon black pepper**

 Assorted crackers (optional)

1. Beat cream cheese in medium bowl with electric mixer on medium speed until smooth. Add broccoli, carrot, milk, onion, lemon juice, lemon peel and pepper. Mix until well blended. Refrigerate until ready to serve.

2. Serve with crackers, if desired.

Makes 2 cups (about 16 servings)

Cherry-Cheese Spread

1 **package (8 ounces) cream cheese, softened**
¼ **cup half-and-half or whipping cream**
1 **tablespoon sugar**
1 **tablespoon cherry-flavored liqueur***
1 **cup fresh sweet cherries, pitted and chopped**
¼ **cup sliced almonds, toasted**

*If desired, omit cherry liqueur and substitute 1 tablespoon milk, plus
1 teaspoon additional sugar.

1. Place cream cheese, half-and-half, sugar and liqueur
in medium bowl of electric mixer and beat at low
speed until just blended. Increase to high speed and
beat until smooth. Gently fold in fresh cherries. (Do
not overmix or spread will turn purple.)

2. Mound cream cheese spread on serving plate
and sprinkle with sliced almonds. Serve with toasted
bagels or plain crackers.

Makes 16 servings

 If short on time, microwave cold cream cheese
on HIGH for 20 to 30 seconds to soften.

Mini Meatballs with Red Pepper Dipping Sauce

- 1 **bottled roasted red pepper, drained and coarsely chopped**
- 2 **cloves garlic, divided**
- ¼ **cup mayonnaise**
- ⅛ **teaspoon red pepper flakes (optional)**
- ¼ **pound lean ground beef**
- ¼ **pound ground pork**
- 1 **cup plain dry bread crumbs, divided**
- 1 **shallot, minced**
- ¼ **teaspoon salt**
- ⅛ **teaspoon black pepper**
- 1 **egg, beaten**
- ¼ **cup vegetable oil**

1. For Red Pepper Dipping Sauce, place roasted red pepper and 1 clove garlic in blender. Process until smooth. Transfer to small bowl; stir in mayonnaise and red pepper flakes, if desired. Set aside.

2. Mince remaining clove garlic. Combine ground beef, ground pork, ¼ cup bread crumbs, shallot, garlic, salt and black pepper in medium bowl. Add egg; blend well.

3. Spread the remaining ¾ cup bread crumbs on large plate. Form meat mixture into 32 to 36 (1-inch) meatballs. Roll meatballs in bread crumbs.

4. Heat oil in 12-inch skillet over medium-high heat. Add meatballs in batches; cook 8 minutes, turning frequently until browned on all sides and meatballs are cooked through (160°F). Drain on paper towels. Serve with Red Pepper Dipping Sauce.

Makes 8 or 9 servings

Note: The dipping sauce may be prepared and refrigerated up to 4 hours in advance. Allow the sauce to return to room temperature before serving.

 Tip Some supermarkets sell a meatloaf blend of half beef and half pork; use ½ pound of the blend. Or, if desired, use all pork in this recipe.

Quick & Easy Hummus

1 **clove garlic, peeled**
1 **can (about 15 ounces) chickpeas, rinsed and drained**
2 **tablespoons torn fresh mint leaves (optional)**
2 **tablespoons olive oil**
2 **tablespoons lemon juice**
2 **teaspoons dark sesame oil**
½ **teaspoon salt**
⅛ **teaspoon ground red pepper** *or* ¼ **teaspoon hot pepper sauce**

With motor running, drop garlic clove through feed tube of food processor. Add remaining ingredients to food processor. Cover; process until hummus is well combined and is desired consistency (the longer the hummus is processed the smoother the texture).

Makes 4 servings

Serving Suggestion: Serve with vegetable dippers or pita wedges.

Tip Leftover hummus may be covered and refrigerated up to 1 week. Hummus makes a great sandwich spread for pitas.

Three-Cheese Pecan Roll

1 **can (8 ounces) crushed pineapple in heavy syrup, drained**

2 **cups pecan pieces, toasted* and divided**

1 **package (8 ounces) cream cheese, softened**

2 **cups (8 ounces) finely shredded sharp Cheddar cheese**

¾ **cup crumbled blue cheese**

2 **tablespoons Worcestershire sauce (optional)**

1 **teaspoon sugar**

½ **teaspoon red pepper flakes**

Whole grain crackers

*To toast pecans, spread in single layer in heavy skillet. Cook over medium heat 1 to 2 minutes or until nuts are lightly browned, stirring frequently. Remove from skillet immediately. Cool before using.

1. Combine drained pineapple, 1 cup pecans, cream cheese, Cheddar cheese, blue cheese, Worcestershire sauce, if desired, sugar and red pepper flakes in large bowl.

2. Shape mixture into 2 balls or rolls; roll in remaining pecans to coat. Cover with plastic wrap. Freeze 30 minutes or refrigerate 2 hours or until firm. Serve with whole grain crackers.

Makes 2 cheese balls or rolls

7-Layer Dip

1 **package (3 ounces) ramen noodles, any flavor, crushed***

2 **tablespoons dried taco seasoning mix**

3 **ripe avocados, diced**

1 **jalapeño pepper, finely chopped****

2 **tablespoons finely chopped fresh cilantro**

2 **tablespoons lime juice**

1 **clove garlic, minced**

½ **teaspoon salt**

1 **can (about 15 ounces) refried beans**

1 **container (16 ounces) sour cream**

2 **cups (8 ounces) shredded Mexican Cheddar-Jack cheese**

2 **medium tomatoes, diced**

3 **green onions, thinly sliced**

Tortilla chips

*Discard seasoning packet.

**Jalapeño peppers can sting and irritate the skin, so wear rubber gloves when handling peppers and do not touch your eyes.

1. Combine noodles with taco seasoning mix in medium bowl; mix well.

2. Mash avocados, jalapeño pepper, cilantro, lime juice, garlic and salt in large bowl.

3. Spread refried beans in bottom of 8-inch glass baking dish. Layer sour cream, noodles, avocado mixture, cheese, tomatoes and green onions evenly over beans. Serve immediately or cover and refrigerate for up to 8 hours. Serve with tortilla chips.

Makes 10 servings

Pumpkin Seed Spread

1 **cup shelled raw pumpkin seeds**
2½ **tablespoons honey or agave syrup**
½ **teaspoon ground cinnamon**
¼ **teaspoon salt**
2 **to 4 tablespoons olive or vegetable oil**

1. Preheat oven to 350°F. Spread pumpkin seeds in single layer on ungreased baking sheet. Bake 8 to 10 minutes or until golden brown, stirring occasionally. Cool completely.

2. Place pumpkin seeds in food processor; pulse until finely ground and powdery. Add honey, cinnamon and salt; process with on/off pulses until combined. With motor running, slowly add oil; process 3 to 4 minutes or until smooth paste forms.

Makes about ¾ cup (about 6 servings)

Serving Suggestion: Use this spread like peanut butter. Try it with jam on rice crackers. Or for a fun, kid-friendly snack, serve it on celery sticks with raisins.

39

Roasted Red Pepper Dip

2 **cups crumbled feta cheese**
2 **tablespoons garlic olive oil**
¼ **teaspoon black pepper**
1 **cup roasted red peppers**
   Pita chips or cut-up vegetables

1. Process cheese, oil and black pepper in food processor 1 minute or until smooth.

2. Add red peppers. Process 10 to 15 seconds or until mixed but not puréed. Serve with pita chips or vegetables.

Makes 8 to 12 servings

Creamy Cashew Spread

1   **cup raw cashew nuts**
2   **tablespoons lemon juice**
1   **tablespoon tahini**
½   **teaspoon salt**
½   **teaspoon black pepper**
2   **teaspoons minced fresh herbs, such as basil, parsley or oregano (optional)**
    Assorted bread toasts and/or crackers

1. Rinse cashews and place in medium bowl. Cover with water by at least 2 inches. Soak 4 hours or overnight. Drain cashews, reserving soaking water.

2. Place cashews, 2 tablespoons reserved water, lemon juice, tahini, salt and pepper in food processor or blender; process several minutes or until smooth. Add additional water, 1 tablespoon at a time, until desired consistency is reached.

3. Cover and refrigerate until ready to serve. Stir in herbs, if desired, just before serving. Serve with assorted bread toasts and/or crackers.

Makes about ½ cup (6 servings)

Tip Use as a spread or dip for hors d'oeuvres, or as a sandwich spread or pasta topping. Thin with additional liquid as needed.

Spider Web Dip

Spooky Tortilla Chips (recipe follows)
1 **package (8 ounces) reduced-fat cream cheese, softened**
1 **jar (8 ounces) salsa**
½ **cup prepared guacamole**
2 **tablespoons fat-free sour cream**

1. Prepare Spooky Tortilla Chips; set aside.

2. Place cream cheese and salsa in blender or food processor; blend until almost smooth.

3. Spread cream cheese mixture on round serving dish or pie plate; smooth guacamole over top, leaving ½-inch border. Place sour cream in small resealable food storage bag; seal bag. Cut off tiny corner of bag; pipe sour cream in spiral shape over guacamole. Run tip of knife through sour cream to make "spider web." Serve with Spooky Tortilla Chips.

**Makes 8 servings
(5 tablespoons dip and 7 chips each)**

Spooky Tortilla Chips

Olive oil cooking spray
2 **packages (12 ounces each) (8-inch) plain or flavored flour tortillas**
Salt to taste

1. Preheat oven to 350°F. Spray baking sheet with cooking spray.

2. Using 3-inch Halloween cookie cutters, cut tortillas, one at a time, into shapes. Discard scraps.

3. Lightly spray tortilla shapes with cooking spray. Place on prepared baking sheet and sprinkle with salt.

4. Bake 5 to 7 minutes or until edges begin to brown. Remove to wire rack to cool.

Makes about 60 chips

Impressive Spinach Dip Appetizers

Prep Time: 30 minutes   **Chill Time:** 2 hours

1   **container (16 ounces) sour cream**
1   **cup HELLMANN'S® or BEST FOODS® Real Mayonnaise**
1   **package (10 ounces) frozen chopped spinach, cooked, cooled and squeezed dry**
1   **can (8 ounces) water chestnuts, drained and chopped (optional)**
1   **package KNORR® Vegetable recipe mix**
3   **green onions, chopped (optional)**
    Prebaked phyllo cups, sliced cucumbers, endive and/or cherry tomatoes

1. Combine sour cream, HELLMANN'S® or BEST FOODS® Real Mayonnaise, spinach, water chestnuts, KNORR® Vegetable recipe mix and green onions.

2. Cover and chill about 2 hours. Serve in phyllo cups or on vegetables.

Makes 4 cups dip

Wasabi Cream Cheese Spread

8 **ounces low-fat cream cheese, softened**
1 **tablespoon prepared wasabi paste**
2 **tablespoons fresh lime juice**
2 **teaspoons rice vinegar**
2 **tablespoons frozen shelled edamame, thawed**
2 **tablespoons chopped green onion, plus additional for garnish**
  Rice crackers

1. Combine cream cheese, wasabi paste, lime juice and vinegar in small bowl; mix well. Fold in edamame and 2 tablespoons green onion.

2. Serve immediately or cover and refrigerate until ready to serve. Garnish with additional green onion. Serve with rice crackers.

Makes 1 cup (about 8 servings)

Tzatziki Cucumber Dip with Crudités

Prep Time: 15 minutes   **Chill Time:** 2 hours

Dip

- 1 **cup peeled diced English cucumber**
- 2 **cups plain Greek yogurt**
  Freshly grated peel of 1 lemon
- 3 **tablespoons fresh lemon juice**
- 2½ **tablespoons minced fresh mint**
- 2 **tablespoons extra virgin olive oil**
- 1 **tablespoon minced garlic**
- 2 **teaspoons sea salt**
- 1½ **teaspoons white wine vinegar**

Crudités

- **Baby carrots**
- **Grape tomatoes**
- **Green onions, trimmed**
- **Zucchini, cut into 2 × ⅜-inch pieces**
- **Bell peppers, cut into 2 × ⅜-inch pieces**

1. Wrap cucumber in clean dish towel. Twist towel to squeeze juice from cucumber; discard juice.

2. Combine cucumber with yogurt, lemon peel, lemon juice, mint, oil, garlic, salt and vinegar in medium bowl; mix well. Refrigerate, covered, at least 2 hours.

3. Place dip in serving bowl. Serve with vegetables.

Makes 10 servings

Caramelized Onion & Walnut Blue Cheese Spread

1 **envelope WISH-BONE® Super Creamy Blue Cheese Dressing & Seasoning Mix**
1 **cup mayonnaise**
½ **cup sour cream**
1 **cup caramelized onions**
2 **tablespoons finely chopped fresh parsley**
½ **cup walnuts. divided**

1. Combine WISH-BONE® Super Creamy Blue Cheese Dressing & Seasoning Mix, mayonnaise, sour cream, caramelized onions, parsley and ¼ cup chopped walnuts. Cover and refrigerate 30 minutes.

2. Stir and top with remaining ¼ cup chopped walnuts before serving. Serve with crackers or your favorite dippers!

Makes 2 cups

Cinnamon Raisin Spread

1½ **cups low-fat cream cheese**
½ **cup cottage cheese, drained**
1 **teaspoon ground cinnamon**
2 **tablespoons IDEAL® No Calorie Sweetener**
½ **teaspoon vanilla**
½ **cup raisins**

1. Place cream cheese, cottage cheese, cinnamon, IDEAL® and vanilla in food processor. Blend until smooth. Transfer to medium bowl.

2. Stir in raisins; cover and chill in refrigerator until serving.

Makes 32 (1-tablespoon) servings

Vegetable Guacamole

Prep Time: 10 minutes

- 3 **medium avocados, mashed**
- 1 **package KNORR® Vegetable recipe mix**
- ¼ **cup coarsely chopped canned jalapeño peppers**
- 3 **tablespoons chopped fresh cilantro**
- 1 **tablespoon lime juice**

Combine all ingredients in small bowl; chill if desired. Garnish, if desired, with chopped green onion and serve with tortilla chips or your favorite dippers.

Makes 3 cups dip

Serving Suggestion: A colorful twist on the traditional, this guacamole works well as a dip or an accompaniment to tacos and burritos.

Layered Mexican Dip

1 **package (8 ounces) cream cheese, softened**
1 **tablespoon plus 1 teaspoon taco seasoning mix**
1 **cup canned black beans**
1 **cup salsa**
1 **cup shredded lettuce**
1 **cup (4 ounces) shredded Cheddar cheese**
½ **cup chopped green onions**
2 **tablespoons sliced pitted black olives**
 Tortilla chips

1. Combine cream cheese and seasoning mix in small bowl. Spread on bottom of 9-inch pie plate.

2. Layer black beans, salsa, lettuce, cheese, green onions and olives over cream cheese mixture. Refrigerate until ready to serve. Serve with tortilla chips.

Makes 10 servings

Swimming Tuna Dip

- 1 **cup low-fat (1%) cottage cheese**
- 1 **tablespoon reduced-fat mayonnaise**
- 1 **tablespoon lemon juice**
- 2 **teaspoons dry ranch-style salad dressing mix**
- 1 **can (3 ounces) chunk white tuna packed in water, drained and flaked**
- 2 **tablespoons sliced green onion or chopped celery**
- 1 **teaspoon dried parsley flakes**
- 1 **package (12 ounces) peeled baby carrots**

1. Combine cottage cheese, mayonnaise, lemon juice and salad dressing mix in food processor or blender. Cover and blend until smooth.

2. Combine tuna, green onion and parsley in small bowl. Stir in cottage cheese mixture. Serve with carrots.

Makes 4 servings

51

Smoked Salmon Dip

- **4 ounces smoked salmon**
- **1 container (8 ounces) whipped cream cheese**
- **½ cup finely chopped tomatoes**
- **¼ cup minced green onions**
- **2 teaspoons capers, drained**
- **Unsalted pretzel crackers**

1. Finely chop salmon or process in food processor until minced.

2. Place salmon in medium bowl. Stir in cream cheese, tomatoes, green onions and capers; mix well. Serve with pretzel crackers.

Makes 1¾ cups (about 12 servings)

Notes: Don't use top-quality smoked salmon in this recipe; less expensive salmon works well.
The dip can be prepared 1 day in advance, covered with plastic wrap and refrigerated.

Hint of Honey Pumpkin Spread

Prep Time: 5 minutes

1 **package (8 ounces) ⅓ less fat cream cheese (Neufchâtel), at room temperature**
½ **cup LIBBY'S® 100% Pure Pumpkin**
2 **tablespoons honey**
⅛ **teaspoon ground cinnamon**

STIR cream cheese, pumpkin, honey and cinnamon in medium bowl for 1 minute or until smooth. Serve immediately or refrigerate in tightly covered container for up to 4 days.

SERVE with apple slices or whole wheat crackers.

Makes 10 servings (2 tablespoons each)

Creamy Dill Cheese Spread

- **2 tablespoons reduced-fat cream cheese with herbs and garlic**
- **1 tablespoon reduced-fat mayonnaise**
- **1 tablespoon reduced-fat sour cream**
- **1 to 2 teaspoons chopped fresh dill**
- **⅛ teaspoon salt (optional)**
- **24 garlic-flavored melba rounds**

1. Combine cream cheese, mayonnaise, sour cream, dill and salt, if desired, in small bowl. Cover with plastic wrap; refrigerate 1 hour.

2. To serve, top each melba round with ½ teaspoon spread.

Makes 4 servings

Bacon Blue Cheese Dip

- 1 **envelope WISH-BONE® Super Creamy Blue Cheese Dressing & Seasoning Mix**
- 1 **cup nonfat plain Greek yogurt**
- 1 **small tomato, chopped**
- 2 **tablespoons thinly sliced fresh basil leaves**
- 4 **slices bacon, crisp-cooked and crumbled**

Combine all ingredients in medium bowl. Cover and refrigerate 30 minutes. Stir and serve with your favorite dippers.

Makes 2 cups

Monster Mash Spread

1 **package (8 ounces) cream cheese, softened**
2 **cups (8 ounces) shredded Monterey Jack cheese with jalapeño peppers**
½ **cup chopped green bell pepper**
¼ **cup finely chopped green onions**
Green Onion Curls (recipe follows, optional)
Assorted crackers

1. Line 8- or 9-inch round cake pan with foil. Spray with nonstick cooking spray; set aside.

2. Combine cream cheese, Monterey Jack cheese, bell pepper and chopped green onions in medium bowl; mix well. Spoon into prepared pan; press mixture evenly into pan. Cover; refrigerate 1 to 2 hours or overnight.

3. When ready to serve, invert pan onto large platter or serving tray; remove pan. Discard foil. Garnish with Green Onion Curls, if desired. Serve with crackers.

Makes 2 cups spread

Variation: Substitute shredded Cheddar cheese for Monterey Jack cheese with jalapeño peppers. Drain 1 can (4 ounces) chopped green chiles and stir into cheese mixture before spreading into prepared pan.

Green Onion Curls

3 **to 4 green onions (tops only)**

Using scissors or small knife, cut each green onion lengthwise into long, narrow strips; place in bowl of ice water. Refrigerate until strips are curled, about 2 hours or overnight.

Creamy Hot South-of-the-Border Dip

3 **cups low-fat plain yogurt, drained***

1 **can (4 ounces) green chiles, drained and chopped**

¼ **cup salsa**

¼ **cup finely chopped fresh cilantro**

¼ **cup finely chopped green onions**

1 **tablespoon lime juice**

1 **teaspoon dried oregano**

1 **teaspoon ground cumin**

⅛ **teaspoon salt**

⅛ **teaspoon black pepper**

6 **cups assorted cut-up vegetables, such as baby carrots, cauliflower or broccoli florets, celery sticks, grape tomatoes, cucumbers, zucchini sticks**

*Place yogurt in a coffee filter or cheesecloth-lined sieve over a bowl and let stand for 3 hours to drain.

1. Combine yogurt, chiles, salsa, cilantro, green onions, lime juice, oregano and cumin in medium bowl. Cover and refrigerate 15 minutes. Stir in salt and pepper, if desired.

2. Serve dip with vegetables.

Makes 6 servings

Olive & Sun-Dried Tomato Spread

Prep Time: 10 minutes

- **1 cup pitted kalamata or oil-cured olives**
- **½ cup sun-dried tomatoes packed in oil**
- **1 cup chopped walnuts**
- **¾ cup HELLMANN'S® or BEST FOODS® Mayonnaise Dressing with Extra Virgin Olive Oil**
- **Crackers or toasted bread rounds (optional)**

Pulse all ingredients in food processor until well blended, but not puréed. Chill at least 30 minutes. Serve with crackers or toasted bread rounds.

Makes 2 cups

Make Ahead: Because the flavor is even better after 24 hours, this is a great make-ahead recipe.

 The olives, sun-dried tomatoes and walnuts can be finely chopped by hand instead of using a food processor, if desired.

Harvest Sticks with Vegetable Dip

1 **container (8 ounces) cream cheese with chives spread, softened**

1 **cup sour cream**

$1/3$ **cup finely chopped cucumber**

2 **tablespoons chopped fresh parsley**

2 **tablespoons dry minced onion *or* $1/4$ cup finely chopped fresh onion**

1 **clove garlic, minced**

$1/4$ **teaspoon salt**

$1/2$ **teaspoon curry powder (optional)**

6 **large carrots, peeled**

3 **medium zucchini**

Tan raffia

1. Beat cream cheese in small bowl until fluffy; blend in sour cream. Stir in cucumber, parsley, onion, garlic and salt. Add curry powder, if desired. Spoon into small serving bowl; cover. Refrigerate 1 hour or until serving time.

2. Just before serving, cut carrots lengthwise into thin strips; gather into bundles. Tie raffia around bundles to hold in place. Repeat with zucchini.

3. Place bowl of dip on serving tray; garnish, if desired. Surround with bundles of carrots and zucchini.

Makes about 2 cups dip

Note: The vegetable bundles can be made ahead of time. Cut vegetables as directed. Place carrots in medium bowl; cover with cold water. Refrigerate until ready to use. Place zucchini sticks in small resealable plastic food storage bag and refrigerate until ready to use. Just before serving, gather vegetables into bundles and tie with raffia as directed.

Roasted Garlic Spread with Three Cheeses

- 2 **medium heads garlic**
- 2 **packages (8 ounces each) fat-free cream cheese, softened**
- 1 **package (3½ ounces) goat cheese**
- 2 **tablespoons (1 ounce) crumbled blue cheese, plus additional for garnish**
- 1 **teaspoon dried thyme**
  Assorted sliced fresh vegetables (optional)
  Fresh thyme (optional)

1. Preheat oven to 400°F. Trim top off garlic; discard. Moisten head of garlic with water; wrap in foil. Bake 45 minutes or until garlic is softened; cool completely. Squeeze garlic into small bowl; discard skins. Mash garlic with fork.

2. Beat cream cheese and goat cheese in medium bowl until smooth. Stir in garlic, 2 tablespoons blue cheese and dried thyme. Cover and refrigerate 3 hours or overnight.

3. Spoon dip into serving bowl. Garnish with additional blue cheese and fresh thyme. Serve with fresh vegetables, if desired.

Makes about 20 servings

Salsa Onion Dip

Prep Time: 5 minutes

- 1 **envelope LIPTON® RECIPE SECRETS® Onion Soup Mix**
- 1 **container (16 ounces) sour cream**
- ½ **cup prepared salsa**

Combine all ingredients in medium bowl; chill, if desired. Serve with your favorite dippers.

Makes 2½ cups dip

Substitution: Also terrific with LIPTON® RECIPE SECRETS® Savory Herb with Garlic Soup Mix.

Curried Chicken Spread

Prep Time: 10 minutes

3 **tablespoons nonfat mayonnaise**

3 **tablespoons chopped chutney**

¼ **teaspoon curry powder**

1 **can (4.5 ounces) Swanson® Premium Chunk Chicken Breast in Water, drained**

½ **cup chopped Granny Smith apple**

1 **tablespoon chopped, unsalted dry roasted peanuts**

Stir the mayonnaise, chutney, curry powder, chicken, apple and peanuts in a small bowl.

Makes 10 servings (1¼ cups)

Taco Dip

12 ounces cream cheese, softened
½ cup sour cream
2 teaspoons chili powder
1½ teaspoons ground cumin
⅛ teaspoon ground red pepper
½ cup salsa
1 cup (4 ounces) shredded Cheddar cheese
1 cup (4 ounces) shredded Monterey Jack cheese
½ cup diced plum tomatoes
⅓ cup sliced green onions
¼ cup sliced pitted black olives
¼ cup sliced pimiento-stuffed green olives
Shredded lettuce
Tortilla chips and blue corn chips

1. Combine cream cheese, sour cream, chili powder, cumin and red pepper in large bowl; mix until well blended. Stir in salsa.

2. Spread dip onto serving platter. Top with cheeses, tomatoes, green onions and olives. Sprinkle shredded lettuce around edges of dip.

3. Serve with tortilla chips and blue corn chips.

Makes 10 servings

Party Cheese Spread

1 **cup ricotta cheese**
6 **ounces cream cheese, softened**
1 **medium onion, chopped**
2 **tablespoons grated Parmesan cheese**
1 **tablespoon drained capers**
2 **anchovy fillets, mashed *or* 2 teaspoons anchovy paste**
1 **teaspoon dry mustard**
1 **teaspoon paprika**
½ **teaspoon hot pepper sauce**
   Red cabbage or bell pepper

1. Beat ricotta cheese and cream cheese in large bowl with electric mixer on medium speed 3 to 5 minutes or until well blended. Stir in onion, Parmesan cheese, capers, anchovies, mustard, paprika and hot pepper sauce; mix well. Cover; refrigerate at least 1 day or up to 1 week to allow flavors to blend.

2. Just before serving, remove and discard any damaged outer leaves from cabbage. Slice small piece from bottom, so cabbage will sit flat. Cut out and remove inside portion of cabbage, leaving a 1-inch-thick shell. Being careful not to cut through bottom of cabbage. Spoon cheese spread into hollowed-out cabbage. Serve with crackers and raw vegetables. Garnish as desired.

Makes about 2 cups spread

Picante Vegetable Dip

²/₃ **cup reduced-fat sour cream**

½ **cup picante sauce**

⅓ **cup mayonnaise or reduced-fat mayonnaise**

¼ **cup finely chopped green or red bell pepper**

2 **tablespoons finely chopped green onion**

¾ **teaspoon garlic salt**

Assorted fresh vegetable dippers or tortilla chips

Combine sour cream, picante sauce, mayonnaise, bell pepper, green onion and garlic salt in medium bowl until well blended. Cover; refrigerate several hours or overnight to allow flavors to blend. Serve with dippers.

Makes about 1²/₃ cups

Roasted Eggplant Dip

2 **eggplants (about 1 pound each)**
¼ **cup lemon juice**
3 **tablespoons tahini (sesame paste)***
4 **cloves garlic, minced**
2 **teaspoons hot pepper sauce**
½ **teaspoon salt**
1 **tablespoon chopped fresh parsley (optional)**
  Paprika (optional)
  Red chile pepper slices** (optional)
4 **pita bread rounds, cut into quarters**

*Tahini is available in the ethnic section of the supermarket or in Middle Eastern grocery stores.

**Chile peppers can sting and irritate the skin, so wear rubber gloves when handling peppers and do not touch your eyes.

1. Prepare grill for direct cooking. Prick eggplants in several places with fork. Place eggplants on grid. Grill, covered, over medium-high heat 30 to 40 minutes or until skin is black and blistered and pulp is soft, turning often. Peel eggplants when cool enough to handle. Let cool to room temperature.

2. Place eggplant pulp in food processor with lemon juice, tahini, garlic, pepper sauce and salt; process until smooth.

3. Refrigerate at least 1 hour before serving to allow flavors to blend. Garnish with parsley, paprika and pepper slices. Serve with pita bread.

Makes 8 servings

Garlic & Herb Dip

1 **cup light sour cream**
¼ **cup light mayonnaise**
2 **tablespoons chopped green onion**
1 **teaspoon dried basil**
½ **teaspoon dried tarragon**
1 **clove garlic, minced**
¼ **teaspoon salt**
¼ **teaspoon black pepper**
   Assorted fresh vegetable dippers and/or pita chips

Combine all ingredients except dippers in medium bowl until blended. Cover and refrigerate several hours or overnight. Serve with dippers.

Makes about 1¼ cups (about 10 servings)

Curried Honey Mustard & Apple Dip

  1 **cup mayonnaise**
¾ **cup sour cream**
⅓ **cup peeled and finely chopped apple**
¼ **cup finely chopped red onion**
  1 **envelope WISH-BONE® Honey Mustard Dressing & Seasoning Mix**
½ **teaspoon curry powder**

Combine all ingredients in medium bowl. Cover and refrigerate 30 minutes or until ready to serve. Serve with your favorite dippers.

Makes 2 cups

Tex-Mex Guacamole Platter

   4 **ripe avocados**
  ¼ **cup lime juice**
   3 **cloves garlic, crushed**
   2 **tablespoons olive oil**
  ½ **teaspoon salt**
  ¼ **teaspoon black pepper**
   1 **cup (4 ounces) shredded Colby Jack cheese**
   1 **cup diced and seeded plum tomatoes**
  ⅓ **cup sliced pitted black olives**
  ⅓ **cup salsa**
   1 **tablespoon minced fresh cilantro**
     Tortilla chips

1. Cut avocados in half; remove pits. Scoop out flesh into food processor. Add lime juice, garlic, oil, salt and pepper. Cover; process until almost smooth.

2. Spread avocado mixture evenly onto large dinner plate or serving platter, leaving border around edge. Top with cheese, tomatoes, olives, salsa and cilantro. Serve with tortilla chips.

Makes 6 to 8 servings

Roasted Eggplant Spread with Focaccia

Focaccia (recipe follows)
1   **eggplant (1 pound)**
1   **medium tomato**
1   **tablespoon fresh lemon juice**
1   **tablespoon chopped fresh basil** *or*
    1 teaspoon dried basil
2   **teaspoons chopped fresh thyme** *or*
    ¾ teaspoon dried thyme
1   **clove garlic, minced**
¼   **teaspoon salt**
1   **tablespoon extra virgin olive oil**

1. Preheat oven to 400°F.

2. Pierce eggplant with fork in several places. Place on oven rack; roast 10 minutes. Cut off stem from tomato; place in small baking pan. Place tomato in oven with eggplant. Bake eggplant and tomato 40 minutes. Cool vegetables slightly. When cool enough to handle, peel eggplant and tomato. Coarsely chop eggplant.

3. Combine, eggplant, tomato, lemon juice, basil, thyme, garlic and salt in food processor; process until well blended. With motor running, slowly add oil and process until well blended. Refrigerate 3 hours or overnight.

4. Prepare Focaccia. To serve, spread 1 tablespoon on each focaccia wedge.

Makes 10 servings

Focaccia

1½   **teaspoons sugar**
1   **teaspoon active dry yeast**
¾   **cup warm water (110° to 115°F)**
1   **tablespoon extra virgin olive oil**
1   **teaspoon salt**
1   **teaspoon dried rosemary**
1   **cup all-purpose flour**
1   **cup whole wheat flour**
     Nonstick cooking spray

1. Stir sugar and yeast into water in large bowl until dissolved; let stand 10 minutes or until bubbly. Stir in oil, salt and rosemary. Add flours, ½ cup at a time, stirring until dough begins to pull away from side of bowl and forms ball.

2. Turn dough out onto lightly floured surface; knead 5 minutes or until dough is smooth and elastic, adding more flour if necessary. Place dough in bowl lightly sprayed with cooking spray; turn dough over to grease top. Cover and let rise in warm, draft-free place about 1 hour or until doubled in bulk.

3. Turn dough onto lightly floured surface; knead 1 minute. Divide into 3 balls; roll each into 6-inch circle. Make indentations in dough with fingertips. Place on baking sheet sprayed with cooking spray; cover and let rise 30 minutes.

4. Preheat oven to 400°F. Spray tops of dough circles with cooking spray. Bake about 13 minutes or until golden brown. Remove from oven; cut each loaf into 10 wedges.

Makes 10 servings (30 wedges)

Fried Onion Dip

1 container (16 ounces) sour cream
3 to 4 tablespoons Worcestershire sauce
1 can (about 3 ounces) French fried onions

Combine sour cream and Worcestershire sauce in medium bowl until well blended. Stir in fried onions just until combined. Serve immediately.

Makes 2 cups dip

Serving Suggestion: Serve with potato chips, if desired.

Creamy Chive & Onion Dip

1 tub (8 ounces) whipped cream cheese with chives
1 cup yogurt
1 bunch green onions (about 5), chopped

1. Combine cream cheese, yogurt and green onions in medium bowl.

2. Cover with plastic wrap and chill at least 1 hour before serving.

Makes about 2½ cups dip

Serving Suggestion: Serve with fresh vegetables, if desired.

Fried Onion Dip

Creamy Chive & Onion Dip

Hummus &
Bean Dips

Hot and Spicy
Hummus Dip

1 container (8 ounces) prepared hummus
½ cup mayonnaise
2 to 3 tablespoons chipotle salsa*
1 tablespoon minced green onion
Pita chips and/or vegetables

*Chipotle salsa is a canned mixture of finely chopped chipotle peppers in adobo sauce. Look for it in the Latin foods section of the supermarket.

1. Combine hummus, mayonnaise, salsa and green onion in medium bowl. Refrigerate until ready to serve.

2. Serve with pita chips and/or vegetables.

Makes about 6 servings

Serving Suggestion: Use this spicy dip to liven up sandwiches or wraps.

Basil Cannellini Dip

1 **can (about 15 ounces) cannellini or Great Northern beans**
1 **clove garlic**
2 **tablespoons extra virgin olive oil**
3 **tablespoons chopped fresh basil**
   Salt and black pepper

1. Drain beans, reserving ¼ cup liquid. Rinse and drain beans.

2. With motor running, drop garlic clove through feed tube of food processor; process until finely chopped. Stop processor; add beans, reserved liquid and oil. Process until smooth.

3. Stir in basil. Season with salt and pepper.

Makes about 1½ cups

Serving Suggestion: Serve with fresh vegetables or sliced French bread for dipping. Add 2 tablespoons fresh lemon juice with the basil for extra flavor.

Chunky White Bean Dip

1 **can (about 15 ounces) cannellini beans, rinsed and drained**
2 **tablespoons extra virgin olive oil**
2 **tablespoons fresh lemon juice**
2 **teaspoons chopped fresh rosemary**
2 **teaspoons chopped fresh thyme**
1 **teaspoon chili powder**
1 **clove garlic**
¼ **teaspoon salt**
   Assorted vegetable sticks, pita chips and/or crackers

1. Combine beans, oil, lemon juice, rosemary, thyme, chili powder, garlic and salt in food processor; process using on/off pulses 30 seconds or until desired consistency is reached. Cover and refrigerate at least 2 hours to allow flavors to develop.

2. Serve with vegetable sticks, pita chips and/or crackers.

Makes 1½ cups (about 12 servings)

Spicy Hummus with Chili-Dusted Tortilla Chips

Prep Time: 5 minutes   **Start to Finish:** 15 minutes

Hummus

- 1 **teaspoon POLANER® Minced Garlic**
- 1 **can (15 ounces) JOAN OF ARC® Garbanzo Beans (Chick Peas), rinsed, drained**
- ½ **cup tahini (sesame paste)**
- ¼ **cup water**
  Juice and grated peel of 1 lemon
- 1 **packet (1.25 ounces) ORTEGA® Taco Seasoning Mix,* divided**
- 1 **can (4 ounces) ORTEGA® Fire-Roasted Diced Green Chiles**

Chips

- 6 **(8-inch) ORTEGA® Flour Soft Tortillas**
  Nonstick cooking spray

*For a healthier alternative, try ORTEGA® 40% Reduced Sodium Taco Seasoning Mix.

PULSE garlic in food processor several times until pulverized. Add beans, tahini, water, lemon juice, lemon peel and all except 1 tablespoon seasoning mix. Pulse several times until well combined. Pour mixture into medium bowl; fold in chiles.

PREHEAT oven to 350°F. Cut tortillas into 6 to 8 wedges; place in large bowl. Lightly coat with cooking spray. Sprinkle with remaining 1 tablespoon seasoning mix; toss to coat tortillas evenly. Spread evenly on large ungreased baking sheet.

BAKE 4 minutes. Remove from oven; turn wedges over and bake 4 minutes more or until toasted and crispy. Serve with hummus.

Makes 6 servings

Creamy Chipotle Refried Bean Dip

- 1 **tablespoon vegetable oil**
- 1 **small red onion, chopped (reserve ¼ cup for garnish)**
- 1 **can (15 ounces) fat-free refried beans**
- ⅓ **cup WISH-BONE® Chipotle Ranch Dressing**
- 1 **cup finely shredded romaine lettuce leaves**
- 1 **medium tomato, seeded and chopped**

1. Heat oil in large nonstick skillet over medium heat and cook onion, stirring occasionally, 5 minutes or until tender. Stir in beans and cook, stirring frequently, 3 minutes or until heated through.

2. Turn into shallow 1½-quart serving dish or pie plate. Evenly spread WISH-BONE® Chipotle Ranch Dressing over beans, then top with lettuce, tomato and reserved onion. Drizzle, if desired, with additional Dressing.

Makes 3¼ cups

Tip Chopped avocados are a great addition to this delicious dip!

Roasted Garlic Hummus

- 2 **tablespoons Roasted Garlic (recipe follows)**
- 1 **can (about 15 ounces) chickpeas, rinsed and drained**
- ¼ **cup sprigs fresh parsley**
- 2 **tablespoons water**
- 2 **tablespoons lemon juice**
- ½ **teaspoon curry powder**
- ⅛ **teaspoon dark sesame oil**
  Dash hot pepper sauce (optional)
  Pita bread wedges and fresh vegetables (optional)

1. Prepare Roasted Garlic.

2. Place chickpeas, parsley, 2 tablespoons Roasted Garlic, water, lemon juice, curry powder, sesame oil and hot pepper sauce, if desired, in food processor or blender. Cover; process until smooth.

3. Serve with pita wedges and vegetables, if desired.

Makes 6 servings

Roasted Garlic: Cut off top third of 1 large garlic head (not the root end) to expose cloves; discard top. Place head of garlic, trimmed end up, on 10-inch square of foil. Rub garlic generously with olive oil and sprinkle with salt. Gather foil ends together and close tightly. Roast in preheated 350°F oven 45 minutes or until cloves are golden and soft. When cool enough to handle, squeeze roasted garlic cloves from skins; discard skins.

Bean and Bacon Dip

Prep Time: 5 minutes   **Start to Finish:** 20 minutes

Chips

  12 **(8-inch) ORTEGA® Flour Soft Tortillas**
      Olive oil nonstick cooking spray

Dip

  6 **slices bacon**
  1 **medium onion, sliced**
  1 **can (4 ounces) ORTEGA® Fire-Roasted Diced Green Chiles**
  1 **can (16 ounces) ORTEGA® Refried Beans**
  ¼ **cup ORTEGA® Taco Sauce, any variety**
  ½ **cup (2 ounces) shredded Monterey Jack cheese**

PREHEAT broiler. Cut each tortilla into 8 wedges. Arrange on baking sheet; coat with cooking spray. Place under broiler and bake until crisp and golden brown, 1 to 2 minutes per side. Transfer to wire rack to cool.

COOK bacon in medium skillet over medium heat 4 minutes or until crispy. Remove from saucepan; drain on paper towels. Crumble bacon; set aside.

ADD onion and chiles to bacon drippings; cook and stir 4 minutes or until onions are softened.

STIR in beans and taco sauce. Cook and stir 4 to 5 minutes or until heated through.

ADD bacon; stir until well combined. Top with cheese; serve warm with tortilla chips.

Makes 6 to 8 servings

Cheesy Barbecued Bean Dip

- ½ **cup canned vegetarian baked beans**
- 3 **tablespoons pasteurized process cheese product**
- 2 **tablespoons regular or hickory smoke barbecue sauce**

  Chopped green onion and red bell pepper
- 2 **large carrots, cut into diagonal slices**
- 1 **medium red or green bell pepper, cut into slices**

1. Place beans in small microwavable bowl; mash slightly with fork. Stir in cheese product and barbecue sauce. Cover with vented plastic wrap.

2. Microwave on HIGH 1 minute; stir. Microwave 30 seconds or until hot. Garnish with green onion and bell pepper. Serve with carrot and bell pepper slices.

Makes 4 servings

Hummus with Garlic Pita Chips

Prep Time: 5 minutes   **Start to Finish:** 15 minutes

Hummus

- 2 tablespoons POLANER® Chopped Garlic
- ¼ cup fresh cilantro
- 1 (16-ounce) can chickpeas, drained
- ¼ cup CREAM OF WHEAT® Hot Cereal (Instant, 1-minute, 2½-minute or 10-minute cook time), uncooked
- 2 tablespoons tahini*
- 2 tablespoons lemon juice
- ½ teaspoon salt
- ½ teaspoon ground black pepper
- ¾ cup olive oil

Garlic Pita Chips

- 2 tablespoons CREAM OF WHEAT® Hot Cereal (Instant, 1-minute, 2½-minute or 10-minute cook time), uncooked
- 1 teaspoon garlic salt
- 4 pita breads
  Nonstick cooking spray

*Tahini is a thick, mild-flavored, light-colored paste made from ground sesame seeds and used in Middle Eastern dishes. It can usually be found in the supermarket ethnic foods aisle.

1. Place garlic in food processor; pulse several times. Add cilantro, chickpeas, Cream of Wheat, tahini, lemon juice, salt and pepper; pulse several more times. While food processor is running, slowly pour in olive oil until dip thickens.

2. Prepare pita chips. Preheat oven to 350°F. Combine Cream of Wheat and garlic salt in small bowl; set aside.

3. Cut pita breads into 12 wedges each. Arrange in single layer on baking sheet. Spray generously with nonstick cooking spray. Sprinkle Cream of Wheat mixture onto chips. Bake 6 minutes. Turn chips over; bake 6 minutes longer. Serve with hummus.

Makes 6 servings

 Tip Hummus makes a great spread. Add to sandwiches, pita breads or wraps stuffed with fresh vegetables.

Layered Beer Bean Dip

1 **can (about 15 ounces) pinto beans, rinsed and drained**
1 **can (12 ounces) beer**
1½ **cups chopped onions**
3 **cloves garlic, minced**
2 **teaspoons ground cumin**
1 **teaspoon dried oregano**
1 **teaspoon salt**
1 **cup guacamole**
1 **cup sour cream**
1 **cup salsa**
½ **cup chopped black olives**
½ **cup chopped green onions**
1½ **cups (6 ounces) shredded Cheddar or Monterey Jack cheese**
  Tortilla chips

1. Place beans in large saucepan over low heat. Add beer, onions, garlic, cumin, oregano and salt; simmer, stirring occasionally, 15 minutes or until no liquid remains. Remove from heat. Mash beans with potato masher or process in food processor. Set aside to cool.

2. Spread half of cooled beans in large dish or casserole that is at least 2 inches deep. Top with half of guacamole, half of sour cream, half of salsa, half of olives and half of green onions. Repeat layers and top with cheese. Serve with tortilla chips.

Makes 4 to 6 servings

Variation: Use refried beans instead of whole beans. Pour a 15-ounce can of your favorite refried beans into a small saucepan. Add only 6 ounces of beer and simmer for about 10 minutes. If the refried beans are not seasoned, add garlic, cumin and oregano while simmering. Let cool and proceed.

Vegetable-Topped Hummus

- 1 **can (about 15 ounces) chickpeas, rinsed and drained**
- 2 **tablespoons tahini**
- 2 **tablespoons lemon juice**
- 1 **clove garlic**
- ¾ **teaspoon salt**
- 1 **tomato, finely chopped**
- 2 **green onions, finely chopped**
- 2 **tablespoons chopped fresh parsley**
  Pita bread or assorted crackers (optional)

1. Combine chickpeas, tahini, lemon juice, garlic and salt in food processor or blender; process until smooth.

2. Combine tomato, green onions and parsley in small bowl; gently toss to combine.

3. Spoon hummus into serving bowl; top with tomato mixture. Serve with pita bread or assorted crackers, if desired.

Makes 8 servings

Sideline Spicy Bean Spread

Prep Time: 10 minutes   **Stand Time:** 15 minutes

- **1 can (about 16 ounces) white kidney beans (cannellini), rinsed and drained**
- **1½ cups Pace® Chunky Salsa**
- **2 tablespoons chopped fresh cilantro leaves**
- **1 tablespoon lime juice**
  Assorted crackers

Mash the beans lightly in a 1-quart bowl with a fork. Stir in the salsa, cilantro and lime juice. Let stand for 15 minutes. Serve with the crackers.

Makes 16 servings (about 2 cups)

Kitchen Tip: Recipes that can be made ahead are always a plus for entertaining. Make this spread the day before and cover and refrigerate it overnight so that the flavors will have more time to develop before serving.

Black Bean Dip

1½ **tablespoons oil**

1 **shallot, minced**

2 **cans (15 ounces each) black beans**

1 **can (4½ ounces) chopped green chiles**

1 **tablespoon minced canned chipotle peppers**

½ **cup cola beverage**

⅓ **cup ketchup**

1 **teaspoon garlic powder**

1 **teaspoon onion powder**

¼ **to ½ teaspoon ground red pepper**

½ **cup cream cheese**

½ **cup spreadable Cheddar cheese**

½ **cup (2 ounces) shredded sharp Cheddar cheese**

Chopped green onions

Tortilla chips (optional)

Salsa (optional)

Sour cream (optional)

1. Preheat oven to 375°F. Heat oil in large saucepan over low heat. Add shallot; cook until softened.

2. Stir in black beans, chiles, chipotle peppers, cola and ketchup. Add garlic powder, onion powder and red pepper. Bring to a boil over medium-high heat; reduce and simmer, uncovered, 25 minutes or until most liquid is evaporated, stirring frequently.

3. Using a fork or hand-held blender, lightly mash bean mixture. In bottom of 8-inch pan, mix together cream cheese and spreadable cheddar cheese; spread mixture to corners.

4. Spoon bean mixture evenly over cheeses and sprinkle with shredded Cheddar cheese. Bake 10 to 15 minutes or until bubbly. Sprinkle with chopped green onions and serve with tortilla chips, salsa and sour cream, if desired.

Makes 10 to 12 servings

Slow Cooker Dips

Sun-Dried Tomato Appetizer Torte

3 **cups chopped onions**

3 **jars (about 7 ounces each) oil-packed sun-dried tomatoes, drained and finely chopped**

3 **tablespoons sugar**

1 **tablespoon minced garlic**

1 **piece (2 inches) fresh ginger, peeled and grated**

1 **teaspoon herbes de Provence**

½ **teaspoon salt**

½ **cup red wine vinegar**

1 **package (8 ounces) cream cheese**

Crackers

1. Place onions, tomatoes, sugar, garlic, ginger, herbes de Provence and salt in slow cooker. Pour in vinegar; stir gently. Cover; cook on LOW 4 to 5 hours or on HIGH 3 hours, stirring occasionally. Let mixture cool before using.

2. To serve, slice cream cheese in half horizontally. (Use unflavored dental floss for clean cut.) Spread ⅓ cup tomato mixture onto one cream cheese half. Top with second cream cheese half and spread ⅓ cup tomato mixture on top. Serve with crackers. Refrigerate or freeze remaining tomato mixture for another use.

Makes 8 servings

Notes:

Torte may be assembled in advance, wrapped and refrigerated until ready to serve.

Toss leftover tomato mixture with hot cooked pasta, shredded fresh basil and cubes of fresh mozzarella, or use as a topping for homemade pizza.

Shrimp Fondue Dip

1 **pound medium raw shrimp, peeled**
½ **cup water**
½ **teaspoon salt, divided**
2 **tablespoons butter, softened**
4 **teaspoons Dijon mustard**
6 **slices thick-sliced white bread, crusts removed***
1 **cup milk**
2 **eggs**
¼ **teaspoon black pepper**
2 **cups (8 ounces) shredded Gruyère or Swiss cheese**
  French bread, sliced

*Thick-sliced bread is often sold as "Texas toast" in supermarket bread aisles.

1. Coat inside of slow cooker with nonstick cooking spray. Place shrimp, water and ¼ teaspoon salt in small saucepan. Cover; cook over medium heat 3 minutes or until shrimp are pink and opaque. Drain shrimp, reserving ½ cup cooking liquid.

2. Combine butter and mustard in small bowl. Spread mixture onto bread slices. Cut bread into 1-inch cubes; set aside.

3. Whisk milk, eggs, reserved ½ cup cooking liquid, remaining ¼ teaspoon salt and pepper in medium bowl.

4. Spread one third of bread cubes in bottom of slow cooker. Top with one third of shrimp. Sprinkle with one third of cheese. Repeat layers twice. Pour in egg mixture. Press down on bread mixture to absorb liquid. Line lid with two paper towels. Cover; cook on LOW 2 hours or until heated through and thickened. Serve with French bread.

Makes about 5 cups

Apricot and Brie Dip

½ **cup dried apricots, finely chopped**

⅓ **cup plus 1 tablespoon apricot preserves, divided**

¼ **cup apple juice**

1 **round (2 pounds) brie cheese, rind removed and cut into cubes**

Assorted crackers

1. Combine dried apricots, ⅓ cup apricot preserves and apple juice in slow cooker. Cover; cook on HIGH 40 minutes.

2. Stir in cheese. Cover; cook on HIGH 30 minutes or until melted. Stir in remaining 1 tablespoon preserves. Serve with crackers.

Makes 3 cups (8 to 12 servings)

Firecracker Black Bean Dip

1 **can (16 ounces) refried black beans**

¾ **cup salsa**

1 **poblano pepper *or* 2 jalapeño peppers,* seeded and minced**

1 **teaspoon chili powder**

½ **cup crumbled queso fresco****

3 **green onions, sliced**

Tortilla chips

*Hot peppers can sting and irritate the skin, so wear rubber gloves when handling peppers and do not touch your eyes.

**Queso fresco is a mild white Mexican cheese. If unavailable, you may substitute shredded Monterey Jack or Cheddar cheese.

1. Combine beans, salsa, poblano pepper and chili powder in 2-quart slow cooker. Cover; cook on LOW 3 to 4 hours or on HIGH 2 hours.

2. Top with queso fresco and green onions. Serve warm with tortilla chips.

Makes 8 to 10 servings

Creamy Artichoke-Parmesan Dip

- **2 cans (about 14 ounces each) artichoke hearts, drained and chopped**
- **2 cups (8 ounces) shredded mozzarella cheese**
- **1½ cups grated Parmesan cheese**
- **1½ cups mayonnaise**
- **½ cup finely chopped onion**
- **½ teaspoon dried oregano**
- **¼ teaspoon garlic powder**
- **4 pita bread rounds**
  Assorted cut-up vegetables

1. Combine artichokes, mozzarella cheese, Parmesan cheese, mayonnaise, onion, oregano and garlic powder in 1½-quart slow cooker; mix well. Cover; cook on LOW 2 hours.

2. Just before serving, cut pita into wedges. Serve dip with pita wedges and vegetables.

Makes 4 cups

Reuben Dip

1 **jar or bag (32 ounces) sauerkraut, rinsed and drained**

2 **cups (8 ounces) shredded Swiss cheese**

3 **packages (2½ ounces each) corned beef, shredded**

½ **cup (1 stick) butter, melted**

1 **egg, beaten**

Cocktail rye bread or crackers

1. Combine sauerkraut, cheese, corned beef, butter and egg in slow cooker. Cover; cook on HIGH 2 hours.

2. Serve with cocktail rye bread.

Makes 12 servings

Sausage Dip

1 **pound bulk pork sausage**
1 **package (16 ounces) pasteurized process cheese product, cubed**
1 **package (16 ounces) Mexican-flavored pasteurized process cheese product, cubed**
1 **can (16 ounces) refried beans**
1 **can (10¾ ounces) condensed cream of mushroom soup, undiluted**
1 **onion, chopped**
   Tortilla chips

1. Brown sausage in large skillet over medium-high heat 6 to 8 minutes, stirring to break up meat. Drain fat. Transfer sausage to slow cooker.

2. Add process cheeses, beans, soup and onion to slow cooker. Cover; cook on LOW 2 hours or until heated through. Serve with tortilla chips.

Makes 20 servings

Pizza Fondue

½ **pound bulk Italian sausage**

1 **cup chopped onion**

2 **jars (26 ounces each) meatless pasta sauce**

4 **ounces thinly sliced ham, finely chopped**

1 **package (3 ounces) sliced pepperoni, finely chopped**

¼ **teaspoon red pepper flakes**

1 **pound mozzarella cheese, cut into ¾-inch cubes**

1 **loaf Italian or French bread, cut into 1-inch cubes**

1. Brown sausage and onion in large skillet over medium-high heat 6 to 8 minutes, stirring to break up meat. Drain fat. Transfer sausage mixture to slow cooker.

2. Stir in pasta sauce, ham, pepperoni and red pepper flakes. Cover; cook on LOW 3 to 4 hours.

3. Serve with cheese and bread cubes.

Makes 20 to 25 servings

103

Pepperoni Pizza Dip with Breadstick Dippers

1 **jar or can (about 14 ounces) pizza sauce**
¾ **cup chopped turkey pepperoni**
4 **green onions, chopped**
1 **can (2¼ ounces) sliced black olives, drained**
½ **teaspoon dried oregano**
1 **cup (4 ounces) shredded mozzarella cheese**
1 **package (3 ounces) cream cheese, softened**
 Breadstick Dippers (recipe follows)

1. Combine pizza sauce, pepperoni, green onions, olives and oregano in 2-quart slow cooker. Cover; cook on LOW 2 hours or on HIGH 1 to 1½ hours or until heated through.

2. Stir in mozzarella cheese and cream cheese until melted and well blended. Serve with Breadstick Dippers.

Makes 8 servings

Breadstick Dippers

1 **package (8 ounces) refrigerated breadstick dough**
2 **teaspoons melted butter**
2 **teaspoons minced fresh Italian parsley**

Bake breadsticks according to package directions. Brush with melted butter and sprinkle with parsley.

Artichoke and Nacho Cheese Dip

2 **cans (10¾ ounces each) condensed nacho cheese soup, undiluted**

1 **can (14 ounces) quartered artichoke hearts, drained and coarsely chopped**

1 **cup (4 ounces) shredded or thinly sliced pepper jack cheese**

1 **can (4 ounces) evaporated milk**

2 **tablespoons snipped fresh chives, divided**

½ **teaspoon paprika**

Crackers or chips

1. Combine soup, artichokes, cheese, evaporated milk, 1 tablespoon chives and paprika in slow cooker. Cover; cook on LOW 2 hours.

2. Stir well; sprinkle with remaining 1 tablespoon chives. Serve with crackers.

Makes about 1 quart

Asian Chicken Fondue

2 **cups chicken broth**
1 **cup stemmed shiitake mushrooms**
1 **small leek, chopped**
1 **head baby bok choy, coarsely chopped**
2 **tablespoons oyster sauce**
1 **tablespoon mirin**
1 **tablespoon teriyaki sauce**
2 **pounds boneless skinless chicken breasts, cut into 1-inch cubes**
   Salt and black pepper
1 **tablespoon canola oil**
1 **cup peeled cubed butternut squash**
1 **tablespoon cornstarch**
2 **tablespoons cold water**
1 **can (8 ounces) baby corn, drained**
1 **can (8 ounces) water chestnuts, drained**

1. Combine broth, mushrooms, leek, bok choy, oyster sauce, mirin and teriyaki sauce in slow cooker. Cover; cook on LOW while following remaining instructions.

2. Season chicken with salt and pepper. Heat oil in large skillet over medium-high heat. Add chicken; cook without stirring 4 minutes or until browned on bottom. Turn and brown other side. Stir chicken and squash into sauce in slow cooker.

3. Cover; cook on LOW 4½ to 5 hours. Blend cornstarch into water in small bowl. Stir cornstarch mixture, baby corn and water chestnuts into slow cooker. Cover; cook on LOW 20 minutes or until baby corn is heated through. Serve with bamboo skewers, fondue forks or tongs.

Makes 6 to 8 servings

Swiss Cheese Fondue

Prep Time: 10 minutes   **Cook Time:** 1 hour

1   **clove garlic, cut in half**
1   **can (10½ ounces) Campbell's® Condensed Chicken Broth**
2   **cans (10¾ ounces each) Campbell's® Condensed Cheddar Cheese Soup**
1   **cup water**
½   **cup Chablis or other dry white wine**
1   **tablespoon Dijon-style mustard**
1   **tablespoon cornstarch**
4   **cups shredded Emmentaler or Gruyère cheese (about 1 pound), at room temperature**
¼   **teaspoon ground nutmeg**
    Dash ground black pepper
    Pepperidge Farm® Garlic Bread, prepared and cut into cubes
    Fresh vegetables

1. Rub the inside of a 5½-quart slow cooker with the cut sides of the garlic. Discard the garlic. Stir the broth, soup, water, wine, mustard, cornstarch, cheese, nutmeg and black pepper in the cooker.

2. Cover and cook on LOW for 1 hour or until the cheese is melted, stirring occasionally.

3. Serve with the bread and vegetables on skewers for dipping.

Makes 6 servings

Kitchen Tip: This recipe may be doubled.

Spinach, Crab and Artichoke Dip

1 **can (6½ ounces) crabmeat, drained and shredded**

1 **package (10 ounces) frozen chopped spinach, thawed and squeezed nearly dry**

1 **package (8 ounces) reduced-fat cream cheese**

1 **jar (about 6 ounces) marinated artichoke hearts, drained and finely chopped**

¼ **teaspoon hot pepper sauce**

   Melba toast or whole grain crackers (optional)

1. Pick out and discard any shell or cartilage from crabmeat.

2. Combine crabmeat, spinach, cream cheese, artichokes and hot pepper sauce in 1½-quart slow cooker. Cover; cook on HIGH 1½ to 2 hours or until heated through, stirring after 1 hour. Serve with melba toast, if desired.

Makes 10 servings

Easy Taco Dip

½ **pound ground beef**

1 **cup frozen corn**

½ **cup chopped onion**

½ **cup salsa**

½ **cup mild taco sauce**

1 **can (4 ounces) diced mild green chiles, drained**

1 **can (4 ounces) sliced black olives, drained**

1 **cup (4 ounces) shredded Mexican cheese blend**

Sour cream (optional)

Tortilla chips

1. Brown beef in large skillet over medium-high heat 6 to 8 minutes, stirring to break up meat. Drain fat. Transfer beef to slow cooker.

2. Add corn, onion, salsa, taco sauce, chiles and olives to slow cooker; mix well. Cover; cook on LOW 2 to 3 hours.

3. Just before serving, stir in cheese blend. Top with sour cream, if desired. Serve with tortilla chips.

Makes about 3 cups

 Tip To keep this dip hot through an entire party, simply leave it in the slow cooker on LOW or WARM.

Festive Bacon & Cheese Dip

2 packages (8 ounces each) cream cheese, cut into cubes

4 cups (16 ounces) shredded Colby-Jack cheese

1 cup half-and-half

2 tablespoons prepared mustard

1 tablespoon minced onion

2 teaspoons Worcestershire sauce

½ teaspoon salt

¼ teaspoon hot pepper sauce

1 pound bacon, crisp-cooked and crumbled

Crusty bread and vegetables (optional)

1. Combine cream cheese, Colby-Jack cheese, half-and-half, mustard, onion, Worcestershire sauce, salt and pepper sauce in 1½-quart slow cooker.

2. Cover; cook on LOW 1 hour or until cheese melts, stirring occasionally.

3. Stir in bacon; adjust seasonings. Serve with crusty bread or vegetable dippers.

Makes about 4 cups

Simple Salsas

Pineapple-Peach Salsa

2 cans (15 ounces each) peach slices in juice, drained and chopped

1 can (20 ounces) pineapple chunks in juice, drained and chopped

1 can (about 15 ounces) black beans, rinsed and drained

½ medium red bell pepper, finely chopped

1 jalapeño pepper,* seeded and chopped

2 tablespoons chopped fresh cilantro

2 tablespoons lime juice

2 tablespoons red wine vinegar

½ teaspoon salt

¼ teaspoon ground red pepper

¼ teaspoon garlic powder

*Jalapeño peppers can sting and irritate the skin, so wear rubber gloves when handling peppers and do not touch your eyes.

1. Combine all ingredients in large bowl; toss to coat.

2. Spoon into 4 labeled 1¾-cup containers. Store in refrigerator up to 2 weeks.

Makes 4 (1¾-cup) containers

 Tip This tropical salsa bursting with fresh flavor is great served with chicken, fish or pork.

Avocado Salsa

1 **medium avocado, peeled, cored and diced**
1 **cup chopped onion**
1 **cup peeled seeded chopped cucumber**
1 **Anaheim pepper,* seeded and chopped**
½ **cup chopped fresh tomato**
2 **tablespoons chopped fresh cilantro, plus additional for garnish**
½ **teaspoon salt**
¼ **teaspoon hot pepper sauce**

*Anaheim peppers can sting and irritate the skin, so wear rubber gloves when handling peppers and do not touch your eyes.

Combine avocado, onion, cucumber, Anaheim pepper, tomato, 2 tablespoons cilantro, salt and hot pepper sauce in medium bowl; gently mix. Cover and refrigerate at least 1 hour before serving. Garnish with additional cilantro.

Makes 32 servings (about 4 cups)

Wonton Cheese and Salsa Cups

24 **wonton wrappers**

1½ **cups (6 ounces) shredded Cheddar or Monterey Jack cheese**

1½ **cups salsa**

1. Preheat oven to 350°F. Coat 24 mini (1¾-inch) muffin cups with olive oil cooking spray. Gently fit 1 wonton wrapper loosely into each cup. Spoon 1 tablespoon cheese into each cup.

2. Bake 8 to 10 minutes or until wontons are browned and cheese is melted. Transfer to wire racks. Spoon 1 tablespoon salsa into each cup. Serve immediately.

Makes 24 appetizers

 Salsa adds the unique flavor to these easy appetizers. Whether smoky chipotle salsa or fruity peach salsa, these bites will be a hit.

Tightly wrap remaining wonton wrappers. They will keep in the refrigerator up to 1 month and in the freezer up to 6 months.

For perfect cup-shaped appetizers, cut wontons into circles with 3-inch round cookie cutter. Gently flute the edges when placing into the muffin cups.

Apple Salsa with Cilantro and Lime

- 1 **cup finely chopped unpeeled red apples**
- ¼ **cup finely chopped red onion**
- ¼ **cup minced Anaheim pepper***
- ½ **jalapeño pepper,* seeded and minced (optional)**
- 2 **tablespoons lime juice**
- 1 **teaspoon chopped fresh cilantro**
- ¼ **teaspoon black pepper**
- ⅛ **teaspoon salt**
  Tortilla chips

*Anaheim and jalapeño peppers can sting and irritate the skin, so wear rubber gloves when handling peppers and do not touch your eyes.

1. Combine all ingredients, except tortilla chips, in large bowl; mix well. Cover with plastic wrap; refrigerate at least 30 minutes or overnight.

2. Serve with tortilla chips.

Makes 2 cups

Serving Suggestion: This salsa can also be used to accent a meal of grilled chicken, fish or pork.

Corn Salsa

½ cup **WISH-BONE® Italian Dressing**

1 **can (11 ounces) whole kernel corn, drained (about 1½ cups)**

1 **medium tomato, chopped (about 1 cup)**

1 **medium cucumber, peeled, seeded and chopped (about 1 cup)**

¼ **cup finely chopped red onion**

4 **teaspoons finely chopped jalapeno pepper, or hot pepper sauce to taste (optional)**

1 **tablespoon finely chopped fresh cilantro, (optional)**

1 **teaspoon grated lime peel**

Combine all ingredients in medium bowl. Cover and marinate in refrigerator at least 30 minutes. Serve chilled or at room temperature with your favorite grilled foods.

Makes 8 servings

Oriental Salsa

1 **cup diced unpeeled cucumber**
½ **cup thinly sliced green onions**
½ **cup chopped red bell pepper**
⅓ **cup coarsely chopped fresh cilantro**
2 **tablespoons reduced-sodium soy sauce**
1 **tablespoon rice vinegar**
1 **clove garlic, minced**
½ **teaspoon dark sesame oil**
¼ **teaspoon red pepper flakes**
  Easy Wonton Chips (recipe follows) or assorted fresh vegetables for dipping

1. Combine cucumber, green onions, bell pepper, cilantro, soy sauce, vinegar, garlic, oil and red pepper flakes in medium bowl until well blended.

2. Cover and refrigerate until serving time. Serve with Easy Wonton Chips or assorted fresh vegetables for dipping. Or use as an accompaniment to broiled fish, chicken or pork.

Makes 4 servings

Easy Wonton Chips

1 **tablespoon reduced-sodium soy sauce**
2 **teaspoons peanut or vegetable oil**
½ **teaspoon sugar**
¼ **teaspoon garlic salt**
12 **wonton wrappers**
  Nonstick cooking spray

1. Preheat oven to 375°F. Combine soy sauce, oil, sugar and garlic salt in small bowl; mix well.

2. Cut each wonton wrapper diagonally in half. Place on 15×10-inch jelly-roll pan coated with cooking spray. Brush soy sauce mixture lightly over both sides of wrappers.

3. Bake 4 to 6 minutes or until crisp and lightly browned, turning after 3 minutes. Transfer to wire rack; cool completely.

Makes 2 dozen chips

Apple Salsa Fresca

Prep Time: 15 minutes   **Start to Finish:** 15 minutes

1 **Red Delicious apple, cored, diced**
1 **Granny Smith apple, cored, diced**
   Juice of ½ lime
3 **tablespoons orange juice**
½ **red onion, diced**
2 **tablespoons ORTEGA® Fire-Roasted Diced Green Chiles, drained**
¼ **cup ORTEGA® Salsa, any variety**
1 **tablespoon REGINA® Red Wine Vinegar**
1 **tablespoon packed brown sugar**
1 **teaspoon dried oregano**

TOSS apples with lime juice and orange juice in medium bowl. Add onion and chiles; toss again. Add salsa, vinegar, brown sugar and oregano; mix well. Serve at room temperature, or cover and refrigerate up to 2 hours.

Makes 6 servings

Note: This salsa goes especially well with pork dishes and makes a great topping for salads.

 Tip Dice the apples in very small pieces and serve with broken ORTEGA® Yellow Corn Taco Shells as a healthy dip.

Santa Fe Pineapple Salsa

Prep Time: 20 minutes   **Chill Time:** 30 minutes

2   **cups finely chopped fresh DOLE® Tropical Gold® Pineapple**

1   **can (8 ounces) red, pinto or kidney beans, rinsed and drained**

1   **can (8¼ ounces) whole kernel corn, drained**

1   **cup chopped green or red bell pepper**

½   **cup finely chopped DOLE® Red Onion**

2   **tablespoons chopped fresh cilantro**

1   **to 2 teaspoons seeded and chopped fresh jalapeño pepper**

½   **teaspoon grated lime peel**

2   **tablespoons lime juice**

• Combine pineapple, beans, corn, bell pepper, onion, cilantro, jalapeño, lime peel and juice in medium serving bowl. Cover and chill at least 30 minutes to allow flavors to blend. Serve with grilled salmon and asparagus. Garnish with grilled pineapple wedges, if desired.

• Salsa can also be served as a dip with tortilla chips or spooned over quesadillas or tacos.

Makes 10 servings

Sweet Dips & Fondues

Warm Peanut-Caramel Dip

¼ **cup peanut butter**
2 **tablespoons milk**
2 **tablespoons caramel ice cream topping**
1 **large apple, thinly sliced (24 slices)**
4 **large pretzel rods, broken in half**

1. Combine peanut butter, milk and caramel topping in small saucepan. Heat over low heat until mixture is melted and smooth, stirring constantly.

2. Serve with apple slices and pretzels.

Microwave Directions: Combine peanut butter, milk and caramel topping in small microwavable dish. Microwave on MEDIUM (50%) 1 minute; stir well. Microwave an additional minute or until mixture is melted and warm.

SPECIAL DARK®
Fudge Fondue

2 cups (12-ounce package) HERSHEY'S® SPECIAL DARK® Chocolate Chips

½ cup light cream

2 teaspoons vanilla extract

Assorted fondue dippers such as marshmallows, cherries, grapes, mandarin orange segments, pineapple chunks, strawberries, slices of other fresh fruits, small pieces of cake or small brownies

1. Place chocolate chips and light cream in medium microwave-safe bowl. Microwave at MEDIUM (50%) 1 minute or just until chips are melted and mixture is smooth when stirred. Stir in vanilla.

2. Pour into fondue pot or chafing dish; serve warm with fondue dippers. If mixture thickens, stir in additional light cream, 1 tablespoon at a time. Refrigerate leftover fondue.

Makes 1½ cups

Stovetop Directions: Combine chocolate chips and light cream in heavy medium saucepan. Cook over low heat, stirring constantly, until chips are melted and mixture is hot. Stir in vanilla and continue as in Step 2 above.

Fruit Kabobs with Raspberry Yogurt Dip

½ **cup plain nonfat yogurt**
¼ **cup no-sugar-added raspberry fruit spread**
1 **pint fresh strawberries**
2 **cups cubed honeydew melon (1-inch cubes)**
2 **cups cubed cantaloupe (1-inch cubes)**
1 **can (8 ounces) pineapple chunks in juice, drained**

1. Stir yogurt and fruit spread in small bowl until well blended.

2. Thread fruit alternately onto six 12-inch skewers. Serve with yogurt dip.

Makes 6 servings

Chocolate–Peanut Butter S'mores Fondue

Prep Time: 5 minutes   **Cooking Time:** 5 minutes

½ **cup milk**
1⅔ **cups (11-ounce package) NESTLÉ® TOLL HOUSE® Peanut Butter & Milk Chocolate Morsels**
1 **jar (7 ounces) marshmallow creme**
1 **cup graham cracker crumbs**
8 **Granny Smith apples, cored and sliced**

HEAT milk in medium, *heavy-duty* saucepan over medium-high heat just until hot. Do not boil. Reduce heat to low. Add morsels; stir until smooth. Whisk in marshmallow creme until smooth. Remove from heat.

POUR chocolate mixture into fondue pot or serving bowl. Place graham cracker crumbs in separate serving bowl. To serve, dip apple slices into warm chocolate mixture, then dip into graham cracker crumbs.

Makes 6 servings (½ cup each)

Note: NESTLÉ® TOLL HOUSE® Milk Chocolate Morsels (11.5-ounce package) or NESTLÉ® TOLL HOUSE® Semi-Sweet Chocolate Morsels (12-ounce package) may be used in place of NESTLÉ® TOLL HOUSE® Peanut Butter & Milk Chocolate Morsels.

Dreamy Orange Cheesecake Dip

1 **package (8 ounces) reduced-fat cream cheese, softened**
½ **cup orange marmalade**
½ **teaspoon vanilla**
 Grated orange peel (optional)
 Fresh mint leaves (optional)
2 **cups whole strawberries**
2 **cups cantaloupe chunks**
2 **cups apple slices**

1. Combine cream cheese, marmalade and vanilla in small bowl; mix well. Garnish with orange peel and mint leaves, if desired.

2. Serve with strawberries, cantaloupe and apples for dipping.

Makes 12 servings

Note: Dip can be prepared ahead of time. Store, covered, in refrigerator up to 2 days.

I'm Dreamy for a White Chocolate Fondue

Prep Time: 5 minutes   **Cook Time:** 10 minutes

- ⅓ **cup heavy cream**
- 1 **tablespoon orange-flavored liqueur or**
  ½ teaspoon orange extract
- 1 **package (about 12 ounces) white chocolate**
  pieces

  ***Assorted Dippers:* Assorted Pepperidge**
  Farm® Cookies, whole strawberries, banana
  chunks, dried pineapple pieces and/or fresh
  pineapple chunks

1. Heat the heavy cream, liqueur and chocolate in a 1-quart heavy saucepan over low heat until the mixture is melted and smooth, stirring occasionally.

2. Pour the mixture into a fondue pot or slow cooker. Serve warm with the *Assorted Dippers*.

Makes 12 servings

Maple Mix Dip

1 **box (4-serving size) cook and serve vanilla pudding mix**
2 **cups low-fat (1%) milk**
⅓ **cup maple syrup, divided**
¼ **teaspoon ground cinnamon**
   Assorted dippers, such as mini waffles, graham crackers, vanilla wafer cookies, apple slices and/or pear slices

1. Stir pudding mix, milk, 2 tablespoons maple syrup and cinnamon in medium saucepan over medium heat. Cook and stir until mixture simmers and thickens. Divide mixture evenly among 4 small bowls or custard cups.

2. Divide remaining syrup among 4 bowls, drizzling over pudding surface. Allow cups to cool to lukewarm before serving. Serve with assorted dippers, if desired.

Makes 4 to 6 servings

Chocolate Molé Fondue

Prep Time: 15 minutes   **Start to Finish:** 25 minutes

CINNAMON CHIPS

- **2 tablespoons granulated sugar**
- **2 teaspoons ground cinnamon**
- **6 (8-inch) ORTEGA® Flour Soft Tortillas**
  Butter-flavored cooking spray

FONDUE

- **1 cup semisweet or dark chocolate chips**
- **½ cup whipping cream**
- **3 tablespoons ORTEGA® Taco Sauce, any variety**

PREHEAT oven to 350°F. Combine sugar and cinnamon in small bowl. Set aside.

COAT one side of each tortilla with cooking spray. Cut into wedges; arrange in single layer on large baking sheet, coated side down. Sprinkle evenly with cinnamon-sugar. Spray again with cooking spray.

BAKE 8 to 10 minutes or until crisp, turning once.

COMBINE chocolate chips, whipping cream and taco sauce in small saucepan over low heat. Cook and stir until chocolate has melted and mixture is smooth.

KEEP chocolate mixture warm in small saucepan, slow cooker or fondue pot. Serve with cinnamon chips for dipping.

Makes 6 servings

Sweet Pineapple Cream Fruit Dip

¼ **cup whipped light cream cheese**

¼ **cup fat-free sour cream**

3 **tablespoons measure-for-measure sugar substitute**

1 **can (8 ounces) crushed pineapple in its own juice**

Fresh fruit (optional)

1. Combine cream cheese, sour cream and sugar substitute in small bowl.

2. Place pineapple in fine-mesh strainer. Using back of a spoon, press down firmly to release excess liquid.

3. Stir drained pineapple into cream cheese mixture until well blended. Serve immediately with fruit, if desired or cover and refrigerate until ready to use.*

*This dip may be made up to 24 hours in advance.

Makes 4 servings

Chocolate and Coconut Cream Fondue

Prep Time: 5 minutes   **Cook Time:** 10 minutes

1 **can (15 ounces) cream of coconut**
1 **package (12 ounces) semi-sweet chocolate pieces (about 2 cups)**
2 **tablespoons rum or 1 teaspoon rum extract**
   Assorted Dippers

1. Heat the cream of coconut, chocolate and rum, if desired, in a 2-quart heavy saucepan over low heat until the mixture is melted and smooth, stirring occasionally.

2. Pour the chocolate mixture into a fondue pot or slow cooker. Serve warm with *Assorted Dippers*.

Makes 24 servings

Assorted Dippers: Assorted Pepperidge Farm® Cookies, whole strawberries, banana chunks, dried pineapple pieces **and** fresh pineapple chunks.

Kitchen Tip: Any remaining fondue can be used as an ice cream **or** dessert topping. Cover and refrigerate in an airtight container. Heat in a 2-quart saucepan over medium heat until the mixture is warm.

Vanilla Almond Fruit Dip

2½ **cups fat-free half-and-half**

1 **package (4-serving size) fat-free sugar-free vanilla instant pudding mix (dry)**

1 **tablespoon sugar substitute**

1 **teaspoon vanilla extract**

1 **teaspoon almond extract**

Fresh fruit (optional)

Beat half-and-half, pudding mix, sugar substitute, vanilla and almond extracts in mixing bowl with electric mixer at medium speed 2 minutes. Serve immediately or refrigerate until ready to serve. Serve with fruit for dipping, if desired.

Makes 10 servings

Fresh Fruit Fondue

- **4 ounces reduced fat cream cheese**
- **6 packets PURE VIA Turbinado Raw Cane sugar and stevia blend sweetener***
- **1 container (6 ounces) nonfat light vanilla yogurt**
- **¼ teaspoon grated lemon peel**
- **1 teaspoon fresh lemon juice**
  Sliced apples
  Large fresh strawberries
  Sliced cantaloupe
  Pineapple wedges

*Substitute 3 teaspoons bulk PURE VIA Turbinado Raw Cane sugar and stevia blend sweetener.

1. Combine cream cheese and PURE VIA Turbinado Raw Cane sugar and stevia blend sweetener in medium microwave safe bowl. Heat in microwave on HIGH 20 seconds. Remove and stir until PURE VIA Turbinado Raw Cane sugar and stevia blend sweetener is dissolved. Stir in yogurt, lemon peel and juice. Refrigerate 1 hour or until well chilled.

2. Serve with sliced apples, strawberries, cantaloupe and pineapple for dipping.

Makes 4 servings

Chocolate Cream Dessert Dip

2 **cups fat-free (skim) milk**

1 **package (4-serving size) chocolate fat-free sugar-free instant pudding and pie filling mix**

1 **container (8 ounces) thawed fat-free whipped topping**

2 **tablespoons chocolate chips, finely chopped**
Chocolate curls (optional)

1. Beat milk and pudding mix in medium bowl with electric mixer at medium speed 2 minutes.

2. Stir in whipped topping and chocolate chips until well blended. Refrigerate until ready to serve. Serve with fruit or angel food cake for dipping.

Makes 24 servings

Chocolate Peanut Butter Fondue

⅓ **cup sugar**

⅓ **cup unsweetened cocoa powder**

⅓ **cup low-fat (1%) milk**

3 **tablespoons light corn syrup**

2 **tablespoons reduced-fat peanut butter**

½ **teaspoon vanilla**

Assorted fresh fruit, pretzel rods and/or pound cake cubes

1. Combine sugar, cocoa, milk, corn syrup and peanut butter in medium saucepan. Cook over medium heat until heated through, stirring constantly. Remove from heat; stir in vanilla.

2. Pour into medium bowl. Serve warm or at room temperature with fruit, pretzels or cake cubes for dipping.

Makes 8 servings

 Kids will enjoy eating fruit with this fondue! Mix and match various types. Orange sections, pear slices and fresh raspberries are just a few of the many other kinds of fruit you can serve with this sweet chocolate treat.

Peanutty Banana Dip ✓

½ **cup sliced bananas**
⅓ **cup creamy peanut butter**
2 **tablespoons milk**
1 **tablespoon honey**
½ **teaspoon vanilla**
⅛ **teaspoon ground cinnamon**
Sliced apples (optional)

Combine banana, peanut butter, milk, honey, vanilla and cinnamon in blender; blend until smooth. Serve with apples for dipping, if desired.

Makes about 8 servings

 Try the dip with Granny Smith apple slices or celery sticks.

Chocolate Orange Fondue

 2 **bars (4 ounces each) 60 to 70% bittersweet chocolate, coarsely chopped**
 2 **tablespoons butter, softened**
1½ **cups whipping cream**
 ½ **cup frozen orange juice concentrate, thawed but not diluted**
 1 **teaspoon vanilla**

1. Place chocolate and butter in medium bowl; set aside.

2. Heat cream in small saucepan over medium heat until boiling; pour over chocolate. Add orange juice concentrate and vanilla. Stir until chocolate is melted and mixture is smooth. Serve immediately, or keep warm in fondue pot or small slow cooker.

Makes 6 servings

 Serve fondue over pound cake cubes or leftover cake pieces, or with an assortment of dippers, including strawberries, cookies, marshmallows, orange segments, apple slices, pear slices, pineapple chunks, banana chunks, graham crackers and pretzel rods.

Pound Cake Dip Sticks

½ **cup raspberry jam, divided**
1 **package (10¾ ounces) frozen pound cake**
1½ **cups cold whipping cream**

1. Preheat oven to 400°F. Spray baking sheet with nonstick cooking spray. Microwave ¼ cup jam on HIGH 30 seconds or until smooth.

2. Cut pound cake into 10 (½-inch) slices. Brush one side of slices lightly with warm jam. Cut each slice lengthwise into 3 sticks. Place sticks, jam side up, on prepared baking sheet.

3. Bake 10 minutes or until cake sticks are crisp and light golden brown. Remove to wire rack.

4. Meanwhile, beat whipping cream in large bowl with electric mixer until soft peaks form. Add remaining ¼ cup raspberry jam; beat until combined. Serve pound cake dip sticks with raspberry whipped cream.

Makes 8 to 10 servings

Dark Chocolate Fondue

22 ounces *KOZY SHACK® No Sugar Added* **Chocolate Pudding**

1 ounce unsweetened bakers chocolate, chopped fine

1 tablespoon vanilla extract

Sliced apples, whole strawberries, sliced bananas, pineapple chunks and cherries

Double Boiler Directions:

1. Add pudding, chocolate, and vanilla to a double boiler (use a bowl that fits on top of a saucepot, half full of water).*

2. Stir mixture over medium heat until the chocolate melts.

3. Serve in fondue pot or serving bowl with sliced fruits.

*Use caution when touching the edges of the bowl.

Microwave Directions:

1. Chop bakers chocolate very fine.

2. Place pudding in microwave-safe bowl.

3. Mix chocolate with pudding.

4. Microwave on HIGH 1½ minutes.

5. Stir pudding every 30 seconds until completely dissolved.

6. Serve in fondue pot or serving bowl with sliced fruits.

Makes 6 servings

Index

Acknowledgments

The publisher would like to thank the companies listed below for the use of their recipes and photographs in this publication.

Cabot® Creamery Cooperative

Campbell Soup Company

Cream of Wheat® Cereal, A Division of B&G Foods North America, Inc.

Dole Food Company, Inc.

Holland House®

Ideal® No Calorie Sweetener

®Johnsonville Sausage, LLC

Kozy Shack Enterprises, Inc.

Mrs. Dash®, A Division of B&G Foods North America, Inc.

Nestlé USA

Ortega®, A Division of B&G Foods North America, Inc.

Pinnacle Foods

Pure Via® All Natural Stevia Zero Calorie Sweetener

Unilever

Metric Conversion Chart

VOLUME MEASUREMENTS (dry)

1/8 teaspoon = 0.5 mL
1/4 teaspoon = 1 mL
1/2 teaspoon = 2 mL
3/4 teaspoon = 4 mL
1 teaspoon = 5 mL
1 tablespoon = 15 mL
2 tablespoons = 30 mL
1/4 cup = 60 mL
1/3 cup = 75 mL
1/2 cup = 125 mL
2/3 cup = 150 mL
3/4 cup = 175 mL
1 cup = 250 mL
2 cups = 1 pint = 500 mL
3 cups = 750 mL
4 cups = 1 quart = 1 L

VOLUME MEASUREMENTS (fluid)

1 fluid ounce (2 tablespoons) = 30 mL
4 fluid ounces (1/2 cup) = 125 mL
8 fluid ounces (1 cup) = 250 mL
12 fluid ounces (1 1/2 cups) = 375 mL
16 fluid ounces (2 cups) = 500 mL

WEIGHTS (mass)

1/2 ounce = 15 g
1 ounce = 30 g
3 ounces = 90 g
4 ounces = 120 g
8 ounces = 225 g
10 ounces = 285 g
12 ounces = 360 g
16 ounces = 1 pound = 450 g

DIMENSIONS

1/16 inch = 2 mm
1/8 inch = 3 mm
1/4 inch = 6 mm
1/2 inch = 1.5 cm
3/4 inch = 2 cm
1 inch = 2.5 cm

OVEN TEMPERATURES

250°F = 120°C
275°F = 140°C
300°F = 150°C
325°F = 160°C
350°F = 180°C
375°F = 190°C
400°F = 200°C
425°F = 220°C
450°F = 230°C

BAKING PAN SIZES

Utensil	Size in Inches/Quarts	Metric Volume	Size in Centimeters
Baking or Cake Pan (square or rectangular)	8×8×2	2 L	20×20×5
	9×9×2	2.5 L	23×23×5
	12×8×2	3 L	30×20×5
	13×9×2	3.5 L	33×23×5
Loaf Pan	8×4×3	1.5 L	20×10×7
	9×5×3	2 L	23×13×7
Round Layer Cake Pan	8×1½	1.2 L	20×4
	9×1½	1.5 L	23×4
Pie Plate	8×1¼	750 mL	20×3
	9×1¼	1 L	23×3
Baking Dish or Casserole	1 quart	1 L	—
	1½ quart	1.5 L	—
	2 quart	2 L	—